ANIMAL PLANET

COMPLETE GUIDE TO A
HEALTHY DOG

verything you need to know
o raise a healthy dog

SF
427
.A339
2015

EVE ADAMSON

COMPLETE GUIDE TO A HEALTHY DOG

Project Team
Editor: Matthew Haviland
Indexer: Dianne L. Schneider
Designer: Angela Stanford
Series Designer: Mary Ann Kahn

TFH Publications®
President/CEO: Glen S. Axelrod
Executive Vice President: Mark E. Johnson
Publisher: Albert Connelly, Jr.
Associate Publisher: Stephanie Fornino

TFH Publications, Inc.®
One TFH Plaza
Third and Union Avenues
Neptune City, NJ 07753

Discovery Communications, Inc. Book Development Team:
Marjorie Kaplan,President and General Manager, Animal Planet Media/
Nicolas Bonard, GM & SVP, Discovery Studios Group/Robert Marick, VP,
North American Licensing/Sue Perez-Jackson, Director, Licensing/
Tracy Conner, Manager, Licensing

©2015 Discovery Communications, LLC. Animal Planet and the
Animal Planet logo are trademarks of Discovery Communications, LLC,
used under license. All rights reserved. *animalplanet.com*

Printed and bound in China
15 16 17 18 19   1 3 5 7 9 8 6 4 2

Derived from *The Simple Guide to a Healthy Dog,* originally published in 2002

Library of Congress Cataloging-in-Publication Data
Adamson, Eve, author.
  [Simple guide to a healthy dog]
  Complete guide to a healthy dog : everything you need to know to raise a healthy dog / Eve Adamson.
      pages cm. -- (Animal planet complete guide)
  Revised and updated ed. of: The simple gide to a healthy dog. ?2002.
  Includes bibliographical references and index.
  ISBN 978-0-7938-3737-3 (hardcover : alk. paper)
  1. Dogs--Health. 2. Dogs--Care. I. Title.
  SF427.A339 2015
  636.7--dc23
                              2014039267

This book has been published with the intent to provide accurate and authoritative information in regard to the subject
matter within. While every reasonable precaution has been taken in preparation of this book, the author and publisher
expressly disclaim responsibility for any errors, omissions, or adverse effects arising from the use or application of the
information contained herein. The techniques and suggestions are used at the reader's discretion and are not to be
considered a substitute for veterinary care. If you suspect a medical problem consult your veterinarian.

Note: In the interest of concise writing, "he" is used when referring to puppies and dogs unless the text is specifically
referring to females or males. "She" is used when referring to people. However, the information contained herein is
equally applicable to both sexes.

The Leader In Responsible Animal Care for Over 50 Years!®
www.tfh.com

CONTENTS

PART ONE

A HEALTHY

START

1

THE WIDE WORLD OF DOGS

W elcome to the wide world of dogs! Maybe you already have a dog but are hoping to give your canine companion the best possible life. Maybe you are still waiting to bring a dog into your life but want to make sure you do everything right. Dogs and humans have lived together and depended upon each other for thousands of years, and we've learned a few things during all that history, not only about how to live more easily with an animal who was, after all, once completely wild, but also how to keep our canine friends happy, well-behaved, and in the best possible health.

This book is about making your dog's life—and by extension, your family's life—as healthy and happy as possible. It isn't enough to toss a handful of bargain kibble in your dog's direction a couple of times a day. Keeping a dog healthy, well-behaved, well-adjusted, and a contributing family member takes some planning and some special knowledge, and that's what you'll find in these pages.

Dogs are the most "plastic" of species, varying greatly in size and appearance.

JUST WHAT IS A DOG?

Say the word "dog" and everyone knows what you mean: Humankind's best friend; buddy to your kids; a sympathetic ear; a head to pat; a friend to hug.

But what someone pictures when she hears the word "dog" is anyone's guess. Do you think of a dog as a Golden Retriever or a Toy Poodle? A

Rottweiler or a Shih Tzu?

Dogs are the most "plastic" of species. No other animal varies so much in size and appearance—not cats, beetles, monkeys, or even humans. If we didn't know better, it would be hard to believe that the tiny, quivering Chihuahua puppy you can hold in the palm of your hand and the petite but feisty Yorkie sitting primly on a little sofa cushion are members of the same species as that gigantic, hairy Irish Wolfhound loping across the dog park or that huge furry Newfoundland pulling his hapless owner down the street.

Because dogs are so varied in size, coat type, life span, working ability, and temperament, it's no surprise that one person's Labrador Retriever is another person's worst nightmare, or that "small-dog people" and "large-dog people" can bicker endlessly about the relative merits of an Italian Greyhound versus a Great Dane.

But knowing about your individual dog's type and breed is more than a matter of aesthetics. Different kinds of dogs have many different kinds of qualities, including different personality traits and especially health issues. Small dogs generally have longer life spans than large dogs and are more portable, but may be more prone to a dislocated knee (called a luxating patella) or

Different kinds of dogs have different kinds of health issues.

collapsing trachea (a condition that causes a characteristic honking cough). Large dogs may have more mellow dispositions as adults and are

What's in a Name?
Many breeds are named after their function. Dachshund means "badger dog" in German, and the long, low Dachshund was originally bred to follow this fierce animal into its underground burrow. Labrador Retrievers were bred to retrieve ducks and possibly fish out of the field or water for hunters and fishermen. Scottish Deerhounds were bred for speed in order to chase down deer.

Be Selective

It's always a good idea to visit your local animal shelter several times during your search process. Perhaps the dog who perfectly matches your specifications is waiting for you there. However, don't let yourself be swept away by a pair of big brown eyes. If that lonely dog peering at you longingly from the kennel is of a type that doesn't match your needs, wants, or specifications, chances are the match won't be made in heaven. Keep looking. That dog may be perfect for someone else. You will be most helpful to a rescued dog if you wait for the one you know you'll be able to keep.

generally easier to housetrain, but are more prone to hip dysplasia and bone density problems as well as certain cancers. White dogs or dogs with large areas of white like Dalmatians tend to have skin allergies and are sometimes prone to deafness, while dogs with long bodies and short legs may have spinal disks more prone to injury. Particular breeds are more susceptible to certain unusual conditions, too, from bleeding disorders to stomach torsion to orthopedic, dental, or skin problems. Knowing your dog's breed and the tendencies associated with that breed, as well as with your dog's coat

Knowing your dog's breed helps you build a solid foundation for his health.

Who to Believe?

When you start researching your breed of choice, you might find conflicting information from different sources that all seem reputable. That's because some dog breeds have certain issues associated with them. For example, one Border Collie breed club believes Border Collies should work as herding dogs and never be shown in dog shows, while another equally reputable Border Collie breed club believes that Border Collies can be shown in dog shows and still retain their working abilities. Both are good clubs, both have members who sincerely care about Border Collies, and both have a point. However, health and care information from dog and breed club sites is usually pretty reliable. On the other hand, personal homepages featuring certain breeds can be fun to read with good pictures and interesting links (and differing strong opinions, too), but they may not always contain accurate care information.

Choose your dog's breed based on which traits best fit your lifestyle.

type, color, and size, will give you a head start in designing a healthy life plan for your new best friend.

Besides health issues, knowing your dog's group and breed can help you give your pet the healthiest kinds of food, exercise, mental stimulation, toys, and general care. While your Maltese and your Saluki both need love and care, their particular temperaments and needs are far from identical. Your Maltese would probably rather sit on your lap, while your Saluki probably prefers a luxurious cushion across the room where he can keep an eye on you. Your Maltese probably needs to eat more often during the day, and your Saluki needs more room to exercise.

THE BREED FOR YOU

Long before most dog breeds were "officially" named, groups or types of dogs looked very different. Sporting dogs, like the Irish Setter, Brittany, and Golden Retriever, scarcely resemble sled dogs like the Siberian Husky, Alaskan Malamute, and Samoyed. Pit bulls don't look like Collies, who don't look much like Airedales or wiry Parson Russell Terriers, who are made for barreling through the bracken after a rat. Guardian dogs built to defend property or livestock, like the Rottweiler, Doberman Pinscher, Great Dane, and Mastiff, barely resemble their toy cousins, built for companionship and lapdog duty, such as the Pekingese, Pomeranian, and Cavalier King Charles Spaniel.

Group Dynamics

The American Kennel Club (AKC) and the United Kennel Club (UKC) differ slightly in the groups of dogs they recognize. The AKC recognizes seven major groups:
1. Herding Group
2. Hound Group
3. Non-Sporting Group
4. Sporting Group
5. Terrier Group
6. Toy Group
7. Working Group

The UKC recognizes eight groups:
1. Companion Dogs
2. Guardian Dogs
3. Gun Dogs
4. Herding Dogs
5. Northern Breeds
6. Scenthounds
7. Sighthounds & Pariahs
8. Terriers

Today, breed clubs like the American Kennel Club (AKC) and the United Kennel Club (UKC) categorize dogs into groups according to their original purpose, although different clubs group and name dog types somewhat differently. Knowing the kind of dog you want can help you to narrow the field before deciding on a breed. Knowing you want a terrier or a sporting dog or a companion breed who fits in your lap can make a big difference in whether the dog you finally choose will grow into your family successfully.

Every group or type of dog has certain distinctive characteristics, both physical and temperamental. If you think you want a Labrador Retriever, it is best to know first that sporting dogs such as Labs are very active, strong, boisterous, friendly, and tractable (they like to do what you say), but have very high energy and exercise needs. If that doesn't fit your idea of the perfect pet, you might consider broadening your search to include other possibilities.

Once you know the type of dog that will best fit into your lifestyle, you can narrow your search down to an individual breed or breed type. And again, knowing the group and breed of your pet is also particularly relevant when it comes to making health care decisions for your pet. Sporting dogs, working dogs, toy dogs, and terriers all have certain health problems to which they are predisposed. They also each have unique care needs and preventive health practices that work best for them.

In other words, know your group, know your breed, know your individual dog, and know yourself! That's the formula to ensuring a healthy future for your four-legged family member.

Guardians

Mastiff dogs were large, powerful, and muscular, and are known to have existed as far back as the ancient Romans, where they were

> Guardian breeds are powerful and instinctively protect their owners.

probably used as guardians and war dogs. Many of the guardian breeds evolved from the mastiff types; think Rottweilers, Dobermans, Great Danes, and St. Bernards.

Guardian breeds are still used today for guarding, protection, and work in the military and in law enforcement, as well as for search and rescue. Many pet owners have guardian dogs who are devoted family members who have a strong instinct

Some Examples of Guardian Breeds

- Anatolian Shepherd Dog
- Bernese Mountain Dog
- Boxer
- Bullmastiff
- Doberman Pinscher
- Dogo Argentino
- Dogue de Bordeaux
- Giant Schnauzer
- Great Dane
- Great Pyrenees
- Greater Swiss Mountain Dog
- Komondor
- Kuvasz
- Leonberger
- Mastiff
- Neapolitan Mastiff
- Newfoundland
- Rottweiler
- Saint Bernard
- Standard Schnauzer
- Tibetan Mastiff

to protect the home and family. However, owners of guardian dogs must be assertive and able to control a large dog, not with violence but with firm, consistent enforcement of appropriate house rules and with plenty of early socialization. Guard dogs don't need to be trained to have a guardian instinct, but they do need to be trained to control that instinct and to interact appropriately with other animals and with humans.

Herding breeds are serious working dogs with high energy and great intelligence.

Herders

Herding dogs are typically medium to large in size with thick or woolly coats to keep them warm as they worked outside all day. They were probably used even thousands of years ago to herd and sometimes to guard flocks of sheep and cattle. Herding dogs

Some Examples of Herding Breeds

- Australian Cattle Dog
- Australian Shepherd
- Bearded Collie
- Beauceron
- Belgian Malinois
- Belgian Sheepdog
- Belgian Tervuren
- Border Collie
- Bouvier des Flandres
- Briard
- Canaan Dog
- Cardigan Welsh Corgi
- Collie
- Entlebucher Mountain Dog
- Finnish Lapphund
- German Shepherd Dog
- Icelandic Sheepdog
- Norwegian Buhund
- Old English Sheepdog
- Pembroke Welsh Corgi
- Polish Lowland Sheepdog
- Puli
- Pyrenean Shepherd
- Shetland Sheepdog (aka Sheltie)
- Swedish Vallhund

remain valuable working members of family farms today.

Because herding breeds usually retain their herding instinct, in the absence of a flock of sheep, they may try to herd children, the family cat, or a local flock of ducks. Herding breeds are serious working dogs with very high energy and great intelligence. These dogs must get lots of physical and mental activity or they are likely to get bored and destructive or run away. Because herding breeds were bred to think and problem-solve for themselves, human companions to dogs in this group must be smarter than the dog and able to provide their pets with the stimulation they require for a happy and contented life.

Sporting Dogs

Sporting dogs were used to help humans hunt small game, first by helping lure game into traps, and eventually, with the advent of firearms, by pointing to small game or birds, stopping and sitting (to avoid getting in the line of fire), then retrieving the fallen game. Some dogs of this type probably spend much of their time as companions and helpers to fishermen, "herding" fish into nets and retrieving fish from the water.

The sporting group includes the pointers, retrievers, setters, spaniels, and some of the more all-purpose hunting dogs like Vizslas and Weimaraners. Once the sporting breeds became more specialized, pointers and setters were used to locate the game so the hunters could flush it out and shoot it. Spaniels hunted ahead of their humans to flush game out of the dense underbrush. Retrievers would gently retrieve the downed game. All the sporting breeds were bred to do their job, then sit or stand still to avoid getting in the way, unlike the hound breeds that more actively chase down game.

Some Examples of Sporting Breeds

- American Water Spaniel
- Boykin Spaniel
- Brittany
- Chesapeake Bay Retriever
- Clumber Spaniel
- Cocker Spaniel
- Curly-Coated Retriever
- English Cocker Spaniel
- English Setter
- English Springer Spaniel
- Field Spaniel
- Flat-Coated Retriever
- German Shorthaired Pointer
- German Wirehaired Pointer
- Golden Retriever
- Gordon Setter
- Irish Red and White Setter
- Irish Setter
- Irish Water Spaniel
- Labrador Retriever
- Nova Scotia Duck Tolling Retriever
- Pointer
- Spinone Italiano
- Sussex Spaniel
- Vizsla
- Weimaraner
- Welsh Springer Spaniel
- Wirehaired Pointing Griffon
- Wirehaired Vizsla

The sporting dogs evolved to hunt with humans, and today even those who don't work as hunting companions tend to bond closely with their people. The sporting breeds are usually tractable—easy to train and eager to please. They make active,

friendly companions but need to be kept busy so that they don't become destructive. Because most sporting breeds are larger than lapdog size, they do require plenty of daily exercise.

Scenthounds/Sighthounds

The hound group consists of dogs who evolved to help humans hunt, but in a different way than the sporting breeds. Hounds work out in front of the hunters, who may be on foot or on horseback, to get the game running. English Foxhounds would run in packs to flush out foxes so that their aristocratic masters could engage in a spirited chase. Bloodhounds, Beagles, and Basset Hounds have skin folds and droopy ears that retain scent, making them able to follow scent trails for miles. Scenthounds like these are often used in law enforcement to track down criminals or locate drugs or explosives (although other non-hound breeds often excel at these jobs, too). Many hunters, particularly in the southern US, continue to use hound dogs in the field today.

Sighthound, sometimes called gazehounds, also have a keen sense of smell but were developed to hunt by sight. These dogs are among the most ancient breeds, according to archeological evidence. Many indigenous or native dogs, especially in hot climates like Africa, share characteristics with the sighthounds, and the art of ancient Egypt suggests that Greyhound-type dogs were common at the time.

Some Examples of Scenthounds

- American English Coonhound
- American Foxhound
- Basset Hound
- Beagle
- Black and Tan Coonhound
- Bloodhound
- Bluetick Coonhound
- Dachshund
- English Foxhound
- Harrier
- Norwegian Elkhound
- Otterhound
- Petit Basset Griffon Vendéen
- Plott
- Portuguese Podengo Pequeno
- Redbone Coonhound
- Treeing Tennessee Brindle
- Treeing Walker Coonhound

Some Examples of Sighthounds

- Afghan Hound
- Basenji
- Borzoi
- Greyhound
- Ibizan Hound
- Irish Wolfhound
- Pharaoh Hound
- Rhodesian Ridgeback
- Saluki
- Scottish Deerhound
- Whippet

In general, hounds tend to be less obedient than sporting dogs because they had to learn to hunt on their own, far from hearing range of the hunter. These independent thinkers are often proficient escape artists and will follow a scent or a small moving object with no thought to looking both ways before crossing a street, so human companions of hound breeds must be extra vigilant in keeping their friends safe (in other words, keep that leash on!).

Spitzes

Spitz-type dogs look very similar to wolves and have served as all-purpose dogs, able to hunt, herd, and pull sleds and carts for centuries. Nordic spitz types like the Alaskan Malamute and Siberian Husky were integral to arctic cultures, and Asian spitz types like Chow Chows and Akitas probably served as family guardians and working dogs in rural areas. Most arctic areas in the world have a native spitz-type dog, from Alaska to Finland to Russia to the Arctic Circle.

Spitz dogs can be challenging. They are highly intelligent and bond closely with their owners, but tend to be indifferent to, if not suspicious of, strangers. They have a strong protective instinct and unlike a louder, more obvious guard dog, spitzes are stealthy and quiet in their approach—meter readers and mail carriers beware.

Spitzes were bred to work hard. Siberian Huskies, Alaskan Malamutes, and other sled dog types have enough energy to pull your whole family on a sled, probably into the next county. All that energy must be channeled

Some Examples of Spitz Breeds

- Akita
- Alaskan Malamute
- American Eskimo Dog
- Chinese Shar-Pei
- Chinook
- Chow Chow
- Finnish Spitz
- Kai Ken
- Karelian Bear Dog
- Keeshond
- Norwegian Elkhound
- Norwegian Lundehund
- Samoyed
- Shiba Inu
- Siberian Husky

Terriers

The terriers are native to the British Isles, where farms often had to contend with vermin and where poorer farmers, unable to keep specialized sporting breeds and hounds for hunting, needed small, all-purpose dogs to help tree squirrels and chase down rabbits and other small game. According to some accounts, small terriers were perfect for poaching because they could quickly

Terriers are feisty dogs bred for scampering and barking.

with plenty of exercise and doggy activities like sledding, skijoring (pulling a person on cross-country skis), weight pulling, or hiking if you want your spitz to calm down when he is in the house. A spitz breed without anything to do is likely to get destructive or try to escape.

Keep your spitz busy with lots of exercise and plenty of daily human interaction. Socialize your spitz puppy to all kinds of people and dogs, and you'll have a happy, well-adjusted canine companion. While spitz types tend to be hearty and weather-resistant, and while they love the cold, they won't be happy outside all alone day in and day out, and they are not typically heat-tolerant. They need to stay cool, and they require human interaction.

hide in the farmer's coat at the approach of the rich landowner.

Bred to be small and extra feisty, many terriers have smooth or wiry coats that are perfect for barreling though the bracken after rats, badgers, rabbits, and foxes.

Some Examples of Terriers

- Airedale Terrier
- American Staffordshire Terrier
- Australian Terrier
- Bedlington Terrier
- Border Terrier
- Bull Terrier
- Cairn Terrier
- Cesky Terrier
- Dandie Dinmont Terrier
- Glen of Imaal Terrier
- Irish Terrier
- Kerry Blue Terrier
- Lakeland Terrier
- Manchester Terrier
- Miniature Bull Terrier
- Miniature Schnauzer
- Norfolk Terrier
- Norwich Terrier
- Parson Russell Terrier
- Rat Terrier
- Russell Terrier
- Scottish Terrier
- Sealyham Terrier
- Skye Terrier
- Smooth Fox Terrier
- Soft Coated Wheaten Terrier
- Staffordshire Bull Terrier
- Welsh Terrier
- West Highland White Terrier
- Wire Fox Terrier

Sometimes used on the hunt even today, terriers could tree a squirrel as easily as they could de-rat a granary. A terrier will bark ferociously to pinpoint an animal in its underground burrow, and will probably be happy to burrow in after it in the same way he will burrow under your covers at night (and most terriers are good at convincing their humans that such a practice is perfectly acceptable).

Any human companion to a terrier must be firm, consistent, and patient. Terriers can be obstinate and have minds of their own. They may not like your rules and will continually test their limits, attempting to re-establish their own tiny little autocracy. If you hate barking, consider another breed. While terriers can be trained to tone it down, barking is a part of this group and was an essential skill for their original purpose. No terrier is going to be quiet all the time.

Toy Dogs

While a 2-pound (1-kg) dog probably wouldn't evolve in nature on his own, humans have been cultivating and refining toy dogs for thousands of years. Popular among European and Asian royalty in past centuries, toy (or "companion") breeds were bred to provide their bored and palace-bound masters with affection, warmth, and entertainment. Many of the smallest breeds come from Asia, where miniaturization has long been an art form: the Pekingese, Shih Tzu, and Pug are a few examples. Other toy dogs

Some Examples of Toy Breeds

- Affenpinscher
- Brussels Griffon
- Cavalier King Charles Spaniel
- Chihuahua
- Chinese Crested
- English Toy Spaniel
- Havanese
- Italian Greyhound
- Japanese Chin
- Maltese
- Manchester Terrier
- Miniature Pinscher
- Papillon
- Pekingese
- Pomeranian
- Poodle—Miniature and Toy
- Pug
- Shih Tzu
- Silky Terrier
- Toy Fox Terrier
- Yorkshire Terrier

were designed to look like larger dogs but in miniature form. The Pomeranian is a miniature-sized spitz breed. The toy spaniels, like the Cavalier King Charles Spaniel, are small and snuggly versions of sporting dogs. The Italian Greyhound is a sighthound in miniature, and the Yorkshire Terrier is a feisty, fiery terrier with a lapdog's tiny size and luxurious coat.

Toy dogs are small and delicate, so they aren't ideal companions for small children because they could be injured. Some toys feel competitive with children, but if given lots of indulgent attention and just the right dose of gentle discipline, they can be perfectly happy in a family with gentle older children who know how to handle them. Although your toy dog may be cute, don't spoil him! These tiny dogs can become miniature dictators.

Many toy dogs are overweight from too many treats and very badly behaved because they are constantly overindulged and not required to follow the house rules. Cute and small they may be, but they can also be yappy, aggressive, and destructive. Well-trained, well-socialized toy dogs make excellent companions, particularly for singles, small families, seniors, and the housebound. Because they are so small, they can get most of the exercise they need scampering around indoors.

Well-trained, well-socialized toy dogs make excellent household companions.

PICK YOUR BREED

Once you've got an idea of the kind of dog you want, you can have a lot of fun perusing the different breed possibilities. The American Kennel Club (AKC) ranks dog breeds by popularity (according to how many dogs of each breed are registered with their organization each year). Below are ten breeds that, year after year, have placed highly on the AKC's dog registration list.

Of course, that doesn't mean you *have* to have one of the most popular dogs. An Italian Greyhound, a Dalmatian, a Russell Terrier, an American Eskimo Dog, an Affenpinscher, or a Sussex Spaniel might just be your perfect match.

Many rare breeds, including breeds not recognized by the AKC, make fascinating and wonderful pets as long as you do your research and are prepared for your dog's special needs and qualities. And don't forget mixed-breed dogs! Many mixed breeds are waiting in animal shelters for the perfect human match, and the animal shelter is a great place to look for a new best friend.

Where's My Breed?

Maybe the breed that interests you isn't listed here. What gives? The sidebars listing breeds in this chapter are not exhaustive. There are breeds in the groups mentioned that are not listed, and there are groups we haven't included because different registries and organizations recognize breeds and groups differently. Notably, we did not include the American Kennel Club's (AKC) Non-Sporting group, because the nature of that group is to represent dogs that didn't fit into other groups, and we didn't include many breeds recognized by other registries.

If you want more info on your French Bulldog, Standard Poodle, Chow Chow, or Lhasa Apso (to name just a few Non-Sporting dogs) or a breed the AKC doesn't recognize, like the American Pit Bull Terrier or the Australian Stumpy Tail Cattle Dog (yes, that's a real dog), check online for more information. Choose a reputable source, like the American Kennel Club (akc. org), the United Kennel Club (ukcdogs.com), or the Canadian Kennel Club (ckc.ca).

Also please note that we do not include information on so-called "designer dogs" in this book because these are really just mixed breeds made from two known purebreds. Labradoodles and Puggles are two of the most popular, but you can learn what you need to know about these breeds by learning about Labrador Retrievers and Poodles or Pugs and Beagles, respectively.

Of course, these breeds are popular for a good reason: They make great companions for the right people with the right kinds of lifestyles. Just remember to research your breed carefully before you make a decision.

TEN POPULAR DOGS IN AMERICA
*ACCORDING TO AMERICAN KENNEL CLUB DOG REGISTRATION STATISTICS

Beagle
Everybody loves a Snoopy dog, but Beagles, while affectionate and playful, will follow a scent across traffic or miles away from home. Ruled by their noses and notorious for their barks and baying, this British descendent of the Foxhound remains a capable hunter and tracker, as well as a jolly and affectionate family pet.

Boxer
This strong, powerful German breed was created to be a versatile working, guard, and companion dog. Boxers are easy to train and thrive when their lifestyles are active and their activities include their people.

Chihuahua
This tiny Mexican dog may fit in your coffee cup, but with his feisty, terrier-like attitude, he's ready to take on any dog, no matter how big. Chihuahua owners must be patient, consistent, and vigilant about this small dog's safety and able to avoid spoiling this potentially Napoleonic tyrant.

Dachshund
Known affectionately as the "wiener dog," this German hound was originally designed to follow badgers into their dens. The Dachshund comes in two sizes—Standard and Miniature—and three coat types—smooth, longhaired, and wirehaired—but all Dachshunds love to cuddle with, amuse, and joyfully defy their humans.

> **Keeping your dog well-trained, well-socialized, and healthy builds the foundation for a great relationship.**

German Shepherd Dog

This herding breed is more often used as a police, military, search-and-rescue, and assistance dog. Highly intelligent with a strong protective instinct, this German breed has been popular since the days of Rin Tin Tin but requires an assertive and interactive human companion.

Golden Retriever

The Golden is a sporting dog of similar size to the Lab but with a longer, wavy golden coat. This native of the Scottish highlands is also active, sensitive, and requires lots of love.

Labrador Retriever

This native of Newfoundland (not Labrador) is the most popular dog in America. A medium-sized sporting breed with an agreeable personality and lots of energy, the Lab makes a great pet for active people who plan to spend a lot of time with their pet.

Poodle

The highly intelligent, personable, non-shedding Poodle comes in three varieties. The Toy, Miniature, and Standard are all considered one breed, and all have extensive grooming requirements. Probably of German origin, the Poodle is a capable water retriever and an attentive, almost-human companion.

Shih Tzu

The Shih Tzu originated in China, descended from the older Lhasa Apso from Tibet. This longhaired small breed is heavy for its size, tough to groom, and decidedly mischievous but agreeable with other pets and a master at the game of human companionship.

Yorkshire Terrier

This terrier may be tiny, but don't underestimate the Yorkie's watchdog abilities, vermin hunting skills, or air of self-importance. This British breed has a high-maintenance coat and is easy to spoil, but a well-trained Yorkie who gets plenty of human companionship will make a delightful and devoted family member.

Whatever breed you choose, as long as you are prepared for the particular qualities of your dog and make the commitment to socialize, train, and keep your dog in good health, you and your new pet can have a long and successful relationship together.

2

THINKING LIKE A DOG

Your German Shepherd looks like he's thinking about something. His gaze is intense as he stares out the window. What does he see? What has captured his interest? He turns to look at you, and you wonder what he could possibly be thinking. Do dogs think? Do dogs feel? What is going through that canine brain?

Scientists, particularly animal behaviorists, have speculated on the thought process of the dog for centuries. Dogs came from wolves, right? So doesn't it follow that knowing how wolves behave and treating your dog accordingly is the secret to communicating with your dog? Dogs must want to move in packs, howl at the moon, and chase game, right?

Yes and no.

Dogs may or may not have evolved from wolves thousands of years ago. There is ongoing debate about the exact origin of the dog, who may have evolved concurrently with the wolf, but either way, the two species have been evolving separately for so long that they have distinctly different behaviors.

While dogs and wolves have certain things in common, they have many important differences. Some dogs tend to enjoy hanging around with other dogs, but some much prefer to be the sole pampered pet in a household of humans. Some dogs bay at the moon, but some have no interest in such uncivilized behavior. Some dogs have a high prey drive and like to chase anything that moves, but that doesn't mean they will catch it or know what to do with it if they do catch it, and some dogs don't even notice that squirrel on the lawn. A well-fed dog doesn't need to hunt and would probably rather share your cheeseburger, thank you very much. Then again, other dogs still retain that instinct to hunt.

So how do you know what your German Shepherd is thinking? Does he have an eye on that cat across the street? The flock of grackles in the sycamore tree? The neighbor mowing her lawn? Does he want to play with, beg, chase, fight, or herd those baby ducks in the pond at the park?

Knowing how your dog thinks is just part of a puzzle that you, your dog's companion, get to put together, piece by piece. Your dog's breed is certainly part of the answer. A herding dog is more likely to be focused on his job and on your direction, whether the job is herding sheep or running an agility obstacle course. A toy dog is probably more focused on getting your attention and scoring a comfy spot on your lap, no matter how busy you are. Your Beagle may be preoccupied with the smells coming from the kitchen (or

the trash), while your Siberian Husky may have one thing on his mind: run, run, run! Because your dog is built a certain way and has evolved a certain way, he doesn't think or feel like a human, although dogs probably have some thoughts and feelings similar to humans. His physical and psychological needs are relatable but different.

FROM WOLF TO PARIAH TO PET?

Once upon a time, there were no domestic dogs, or what scientists call *Canis familiaris*. There were wolves,

Personality Puzzle

Like people, dogs have their own, individual personalities. While many Border Collies have a strong herding instinct and are intensely focused on their task, some defy the rules and prefer the couch. While some Doberman Pinschers have a strong protective instinct, a few individuals will be happy to lead the nice burglar to the family silver. Knowing a breed's tendencies is helpful in determining what your pet will be like and what his tendencies will be, but you'll never be able to predict any dog's personality completely. Just like people, you have to get to know them before you can accurately judge them. Then again, that's the fun part of living with a dog!

coyotes, foxes, and jackals but no dogs. Until recently, scientists believed that dogs evolved from tamer gray wolves who tended to hang around humans looking for handouts, but more recent genetic information suggests that gray wolves and dogs probably had a common ancestor—probably a type of wolf that is now extinct. Other dog breeds, such as the Australian dingo and the African Basenji, arose in areas where wolves never lived, deepening the mystery. What we do know for sure is that the domestic dog of today evolved into its current form (in all its great diversity) alongside humans as companions, workers, and helpmates. We coevolved in many ways, turning each other into what we are today. This coevolution has fostered an intense bond that dogs and humans continue to share.

The domestic dog of today evolved into its current form alongside humans as companions, workers, and helpmates.

Some dogs evolved to live near human settlements and live off human garbage. These "pariah" dogs exist today in many countries around the world. They aren't tame, exactly, but they know where the food is, and they don't tend to be aggressive. These pariah dogs look similar all over the world, suggesting that a certain physical structure is most beneficial, in evolutionary terms, to the scavenging life. Pariah dogs tend to be medium in size with short to medium-length coats (often speckled), pointed ears, dropped but slightly curving tails, long legs, and an instinct to stay close—but not too close—to humans.

Meanwhile, those dogs whom humans took on as helpers and companions evolved into all kinds of different forms, from tiny Chihuahua to towering Great Dane. Today, wolves, pariah dogs, and pet dogs all share the same earth but have their separate niches. They all have similarities, but they are not the same. Wolves live in the wild. Pariah dogs live on the fringes of human society. And as you well know, pet dogs live with us. Sometimes they even sleep under the quilts in the crooks of our knees or warming our feet. (Admit it!)

We know domestic dogs are different from wolves in many ways. For example, wolves are extremely difficult to tame. While it can be done, tame wolves are not like tame dogs. They are more fearful, less predictable, and more prone to attack when cornered. Wolves also do not retain the softer, puppy-like features that domestic dogs keep into adulthood (to which humans respond so readily). Wolves and wolf hybrids can be submissive, even cowering. They may bite out of fear. They can also be friendly and playful. But you can never be as sure of what to expect as you can with a domestic dog. Wolves are more likely to rely only on themselves for their survival, and if let loose, they are likely to run away. They might come back, or they might not.

Sure, some dogs do those things, especially when they haven't been well socialized and trained. However, a puppy who is socialized to many different people, trained well, and given lots of human attention is a

Wolves are amazing, fascinating, beautiful creatures, but they haven't evolved to be pets.

much more predictable, dependable, and safe animal to have around than a "tamed" wolf, no matter what the breed. Wolves are amazing, fascinating, beautiful creatures, but they haven't evolved to be pets.

Dogs have evolved for so many centuries to live with humans that they have adapted in ways that make them appropriate and happy companions. When compared to a wild animal, dogs are easy to live with. In many cases, dogs are even essential for human livelihood, whether that means working as a farm hand, hunting hound, or companion.

Yet they are still animals. They don't speak English (although many

> Dogs are happy, even eager, to learn the rules. They want to please us.

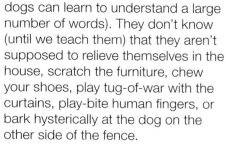

dogs can learn to understand a large number of words). They don't know (until we teach them) that they aren't supposed to relieve themselves in the house, scratch the furniture, chew your shoes, play tug-of-war with the curtains, play-bite human fingers, or bark hysterically at the dog on the other side of the fence.

Dogs are happy, even eager, to learn the rules. They want to please us, they enjoy doing what makes their people happy, and they live for praise, attention, affection, and of course, a nice treat. Dogs will joyfully spin in circles, sit, lie down, shake, play dead, pull a wheelchair, pick up a remote control, fetch a newspaper, or lick away tears. Dogs are made for us as we (one could easily argue) were made for dogs.

In their relatively short evolution into human companion, dogs have also evolved physically into a unique creature, wildly varied in morphology but with some common traits. Knowing how a dog is built is key to knowing how to keep a dog healthy, so let's look at the body of a dog and what it says about dog health and even dog behavior.

THE BODY OF THE DOG

Obviously, dogs are built differently than humans. Dogs walk on four legs instead of two. They

have tails and muzzles, fur and paws. They have a different perspective on the world. Some of them have eyes less than a foot (0.5 m) off the ground.

Think about how the world appears from a dog's perspective. People must look like strange, towering creatures, surprisingly stable on their two legs, hardly victims waiting to be attacked but possibly foes to be feared unless they prove themselves benevolent. Children must seem unpredictable, kinetic, somewhat like peers and yet strangely different with their groping hands. And who knows how your own individual pet will interpret the behavior of all the many other creatures he may encounter during a lifetime: cats, guinea pigs, parakeets, squirrels, crows, strangers, intruders, neighbors, friends, and

Dogs, Not People

It's easy to assume that dogs think like us, and they surely do in some ways, but their unusual vantage, their more highly attuned senses, their different physical structure, and their limited (but not *that* limited) intelligence make a dog's perspective much different from a human's perspective. Assigning human characteristics to an animal (or to anything else that isn't human) is called "anthropomorphism."

lots and lots of other dogs, some aggressive, some friendly, some indifferent, some instant canine buddies.

Even though your Rottweiler might toss toys into the air with his front paws, dogs don't have hands and don't begin to approach a human's manual dexterity. All four paws are primarily for walking, but as puppies, dogs use their mouths in much the same way humans use their hands— to explore their environments. Your terrier can hear sounds in the night you'll never hear. Your Beagle can smell so much better than you can that he can detect thousands of different smells, can follow a human trail for miles, can even detect cancer cells in skin samples and the chemical changes preceding a seizure in the humans around him.

Your Afghan can see a rabbit rustling in the underbrush from miles away and can get there faster than you could on a bicycle. Dogs are very fast. Just try to get ahold of that tiny Yorkshire Terrier if he doesn't want to let you, let alone outrun a Greyhound! These keen senses, high speed, and dexterity, along with strong jaws and sharp teeth, have helped dogs to

Body Talk

The stop is the part of a dog's face that separates the skull from the muzzle. Some dogs, like Golden Retrievers and Cocker Spaniels, have a well-defined stop. It's obvious where the skull ends and the muzzle starts. Others, like Greyhounds and Fox Terriers, have only a slight stop. These dogs have more wedge-shaped heads and the skull flows in almost a straight line into the muzzle. An American Staffordshire Terrier has a distinct stop, while a Bull Terrier has no stop at all.

survive. Dogs can sense danger, run away quickly, or fight if they must. They are also experts at finding food.

But the same traits that make dogs so adaptable also make them vulnerable to certain health conditions. Genetic diseases occur seemingly randomly in mixed-breed dogs but occur in more obvious patterns in purebred dogs. When breeders isolate a gene pool of, say, St. Bernards, certain genetic conditions and conditions related to physiology are likely to become more concentrated, so while mixed breeds get most genetic diseases, purebreds get more of just a few. For example, the strong bodies and deep chests of working dogs make them more prone to bloat, a dangerous and often fatal disease in which the stomach twists on itself.

Your Fast Friend

Greyhounds can run faster than any other breed of dog. At full speed, a Greyhound can run about 40 miles (64.5 km) per hour.

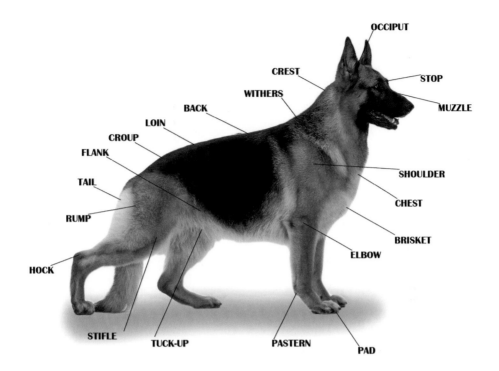

OCCIPUT

CREST

STOP

WITHERS

MUZZLE

BACK

LOIN

CROUP

SHOULDER

FLANK

TAIL

CHEST

RUMP

BRISKET

ELBOW

HOCK

STIFLE

TUCK-UP

PASTERN

PAD

Dogs made to be long and low like Dachshunds and Pekingese are more likely to experience degenerative spinal disks resulting in canine intervertebral disk disease, another dangerous condition that can cause permanent paralysis.

Once again, you can see how knowing your individual pet's characteristics can help you to be on the lookout for certain health conditions. Let's look at a dog's body piece by piece and talk about how different shapes, types, colors, and conditions predispose your dog to certain strengths, and inevitably, certain weaknesses.

WHAT YOUR DOG'S ANATOMY TELLS YOU

Dogs have legs, eyes, ears, backbones, hips, ribs, a heart, a liver, and many of the same organs and structures humans have. But they also have stifles, hocks, muzzles, pasterns, withers, and paws. See the illustration above to identify just what's what on your canine friend.

Knowing something about your dog's anatomy can help you know a lot about your dog's health and potential health issues. The kind of head, face, ears, coat, body shape, height, and even color

can specifically impact your dog's needs, health risks, and care requirements. Let's look at what each part of your dog can tell you about him.

Your Dog's Head and Face

First take a look at your dog's head and face. Some dogs have long, thin heads and muzzles, like a Whippet. Some have short, flat faces with barely a muzzle to be found, like a Pug or a Bulldog. Some dogs fall somewhere in the middle.

The flatness of your dog's face affects how well he breathes, sees, smells, and tastes. Dogs with very flat faces, like Pugs, Bulldogs, and English Toy Spaniels, are called "brachycephalic" dogs. They snore, snort, and snuffle through life.

Because their nasal passages are shortened, they are less tolerant of the heat and will be more susceptible to heatstroke. Brachycephalic airway syndrome is a more serious condition in which the shortened airway passages cause the dog to experience reduced oxygen intake. This condition's symptoms include blue-tinged skin, exercise intolerance, and severe snorting, snuffling, choking, gagging, open-mouthed breathing, and other sounds that suggest difficulty breathing. Other anatomical features that contribute to this condition in brachycephalic dogs are an elongated soft palate (this

> Dogs with flat faces are called "brachycephalic" and have various health concerns.

condition is largely responsible for that persistent snore emanating from your snoozing Pug) and nostrils that are pushed closed due to the flat face shape.

Brachycephalic dogs also tend to have large eyes that can be more vulnerable to injury. Skin folds can cause eyelashes to rub against the eyes, causing irritation. Some dogs with large eyes have eyelids that don't completely close over their eyes, a condition that can result in blindness. They may also be prone to dry eyes. Your vet can prescribe an ointment for this problem. Eyeball prolapse is another emergency condition in which the dog's eyeball pops out. (If this happens, rush your pet and his eye to the emergency veterinary clinic immediately.)

If your dog has a flat face, make sure that he stays cool in summer. And never leave any dog in a parked car!

While some snoring and snorting is typical of a flat-faced breed, make sure to mention it to your veterinarian so she can continue to monitor your friend for problems. And watch out for those eyes! Teach children never to touch a dog's eyes.

Some dogs get cataracts, usually in their senior years, but sometimes even as puppies. If your dog's eyes look cloudy, have him checked. Also see your vet if your dog's eyes look red or irritated. Dogs can get things in their eyes just like people. Some dogs are also prone to a genetic condition called entropion in which the eyelid grows in toward the eye, and eyelash hairs irritate the cornea.

Many breeds are also prone to progressive retinal atrophy or PRA. If your aging dog doesn't seem to see as well as he used to, have your vet check his eyes. PRA causes blindness, but a blind dog can still live comfortably and happily with his family with a little extra care. Less serious is the tearstaining that occurs in some breeds. This staining is more noticeable in breeds with light coats. White Poodles, Bichons, and light-colored Pekingese often have tearstains, which is usually just a cosmetic problem. Ask your vet about products to treat it if it bothers you.

Your Dog's Ears

A Basenji has short pointed ears. A Basset Hound has long droopy ears. A Fox Terrier has ears neatly folded over. What's the difference?

A dog's ear shape is more than a matter of looks. Dogs with long droopy ears are prone to skin infections in the folds of the ear, and dogs with very short ears are prone to ear infections because the inner ear is less protected. Keep an eye on your dog's ears and call your vet if your dog starts to scratch his ears more often. Scratching could mean an infection or a pest infestation. Your vet should check your pet's ears at every annual checkup.

Dogs with large areas of white like Dalmatians and Beagles are prone to

Doggy Dreadlocks

Some breeds have hair that easily works itself into dreadlock-type cords. The Puli and the Komondor grow beautifully corded coats. Poodle coats can also be worked into cords, although most people keep their Poodles in a puppy cut, pet cut, or show cut.

doesn't seem to hear you when you aren't making eye contact, ask your vet about testing your dog's hearing. If you bought your dog from a breeder, ask if the breeder did hearing tests on your dog. These are called BAER (brainstem auditory evoked response) tests, and they are the same tests used on infants and small children.

Your Dog's Coat

Later in this book, you'll read about the importance of regular grooming sessions for monitoring your dog's health. Keeping your dog well-groomed is also important for good health. Some dogs have wiry coats that require stripping to stay in good shape.

genetic deafness in one or both ears. Deaf dogs should never be bred, but they can make fine pets if you are prepared to make allowances for your dog's disability. However, if you don't know your dog is deaf, you can't meet his special needs. If you have a dog with a large amount of white in his coat or you have a senior dog who

A healthy, shiny, and full coat signifies a healthy dog.

Stripping involves plucking dead hairs from your dog's coat with your fingers or grooming tools designed for that purpose. Some dogs have long coats, curly coats, and/or double coats that require frequent attention to prevent them from matting. Mats in your dog's coat are difficult to remove and can attract dirt and pests because they make it difficult to get down to the skin when brushing and washing. Mats usually must be cut out of the dog's fur or shaved. Some people choose to keep their long-coated dogs cropped close to avoid mats, but those who want to keep their Pekingese, Poodle, or Puli in a show coat should be prepared for a lot of attention to grooming.

Your Dog's Body

The shape of your dog's body determines how he will move as well as what kind of health

Large breeds with deep chests are prone to bloat, a serious health condition.

problems he might eventually have to face. Some dogs, like Great Danes and German Shepherds, have deep chests. Some dogs, like Pekingese and Skye Terriers, have long backs. Some dogs, like Dachshunds and Basset Hounds, have both.

Large dogs with deep chests are more prone to a severe health condition called bloat, also known as canine gastric dilatation-volvulus (CGDV) or stomach torsion. Nobody knows for sure what triggers this serious, life-threatening condition, but there is some evidence that it is more likely to result when large dogs are fed only once a day and gulp their food too quickly, sometimes followed by drinking a large amount of water and immediate vigorous exercise. When bloat occurs, the stomach twists, and without immediate medical attention, the condition is usually fatal. Some dogs prone to bloat will experience it multiple times. For this reason, as a precaution especially in breeds prone to bloat, large and barrel-chested dogs should be fed smaller amounts more often—two to three meals a day instead of one—and should avoid vigorous exercise for an hour or two after eating, just in case. In some breeds or bloodlines where bloat is a recurrent problem, gastropexy may save an animal's life. This procedure anchors the stomach in any of several different ways, to prevent recurrence. Bloat is an emergency, and you have no time to wait. If you suspect your dog is experiencing bloat, take him to the vet or emergency pet care center immediately. (Check the "Digestive System" section in Chapter 7 for a description of bloat symptoms.)

Dogs who are longer than they are tall are prone to a different but also very serious condition called canine intervertebral disk disease or canine degenerative disk disease. This degenerative spinal condition can result in rupture of a spinal disk and also occurs in humans. Because long-backed dogs have more pressure and movement on their spines than dogs with short backs and longer legs, the condition is more common in small dogs like Dachshunds and Pekingese. If not treated immediately, a disk rupture can result in permanent paralysis, so don't ignore stumbling, wobbling, yelps of pain when you touch your dog's back, or sudden refusals to move. Call your vet immediately.

Your Dog's Height and Weight

Your leggy, soon-to-be-towering Great Dane puppy and other large and giant breeds may be intimidating on the end of a leash, and they may be big goofy clowns at home, but growth like that comes with a few challenges. Large and giant breeds end up with a lot of bone. If a puppy grows too fast, his skeleton won't develop as well as it would at a slower growth rate, making your big baby susceptible to bone, joint, and cartilage disorders. Rather than feeding your large or giant breed a regular puppy food in his first year, which can be too high in protein and can result in too-rapid growth, feed a premium adult food or a puppy food specially formulated for large or giant breeds. Also feed appropriate amounts of food so that your puppy grows at an appropriate rate and doesn't become overweight. Sure, it's impressive to see a little Mastiff

Large and giant breeds sometimes develop too quickly eating certain foods.

puppy inhaling a huge volume of kibble, but it isn't healthy for him. Stick to the amount of food your vet recommends, and a few healthy treats like baby carrots, blueberries, broccoli florets, plain yogurt, and a few low-fat doggy treats, or use your pet's regular kibble, for training.

The most difficult part of loving a large dog may be the short life span. The bigger the dog, the shorter his life span and the sooner he is likely to age and develop the diseases of aging, like heart disease and cancer. Giant and some large breeds are considered seniors at about six years of age. A Chihuahua may not slow down until well beyond twice that many years, and some small dogs live into their 20s. Giant breeds have a life span of approximately 10 years, some even less.

Small dogs have a separate set of bone and joint problems. Tiny pets like Affenpinschers and Cavalier King Charles Spaniels are more prone to luxating patellas (kneecaps slipping out of place) and slipped stifles (knee joints slipping out of place). Small dogs often suffer from arthritis as seniors and are not tolerant of extreme weather conditions. Your toy dog must live inside the house with you! Small dogs are also more fragile, especially as puppies. A jump from a high couch or the arms of a child could result in leg fractures in a Pomeranian,

Italian Greyhound, Miniature Pinscher, Papillon, Toy Poodle, Chihuahua, or any other small, light-boned puppy.

Your Dog's Color

As mentioned above, dogs with large amounts of white, like Dalmatians and Beagles, are more prone to hereditary deafness. Color can influence your pet in other ways, too. Black dogs are less heat tolerant because their coat absorbs heat. Your black Lab may become dangerously overheated long before his brother, the yellow Lab. Rottweilers look tough but are notoriously intolerant of high temperatures, and small black dogs like Affenpinschers and Manchester Terriers can quickly develop heatstroke on a hot summer day out in the sun.

Light-colored dogs may not feel hot as quickly, but their light coats may offer less sun protection. Dogs get sunburned, too, and can even develop skin cancer. Don't let your white Poodle, your Bichon, your red Miniature Pinscher, or any light-colored dog sunbathe for too long without first applying a canine sunscreen spray (yes, they make it!).

HOW DO DOGS THINK?

You can examine your dog's coat, his paws, his ears, even his teeth, but you can't examine the canine brain just by

looking. While dog anatomy and even dog genetics are well understood, what goes on in the canine brain remains largely a matter of speculation. No one can really say with certainty how a dog thinks in the way they can say how a dog breathes, digests, or heals. However, animal behaviorists do know a lot about how dogs behave and how they are likely to behave.

One of the more convincing theories about the canine thought process is that dogs think in images. Not having language, as we do, but being intelligent nevertheless, dogs probably

> **Dogs remember various sensory cues, such as different tones of voice and the sight of you walking to the closet where the leashes are kept.**

think in a way similar to humans before they evolved to use language, or to young children who haven't yet learned to speak. Dogs have visual, aural, tactile, taste, and smell images from their environments. They remember these images, both the pleasant ones, like you lavishing affection or giving treats, and the unpleasant ones, like you yelling or leaving.

But they don't speak. Sure, they can understand the meanings of certain words. Some dogs even know hundreds of words, and their humans claim they seem to understand the gist of conversations going on in the room. That may indeed be true, but not because dogs possess language. Dogs get the "gist" because they understand the images. They remember that whenever you come home, you pet and praise them. They remember that when you get a certain tone of voice or when you walk to the closet where the leashes are kept, a treat or a walk or a trip to the park are probably imminent. They also might associate an image of the car with an unpleasant trip to the vet or feel fear at the auditory "image" of thunder, yelling, a certain breed of dog, or even a small child, depending on the past imagery associated with that thing.

So what does that mean for our relationship with dogs? How do we use this information for better communication?

Understanding canine psychology is essential for behavioral conditioning.

DO WE NEED TO THINK LIKE A DOG?

Dogs are creatures of habit, and they like routines. They are also smart enough to remember things they like and try to make them happen again, and they remember things they don't like and try to avoid them. Understanding how this works is critical to teaching your dog what you want him to do, as well as what you don't want him to do.

The first key is to understand why your dog does the things he does. Did he chew up your shoe when you were late coming home because he was mad at you? Behaviorist William E. Campbell suggests that instead, your dog didn't get the pleasant image of you coming home when he expected it, so he's trying to get some kind of experience of you in place of the real deal. Did he defecate on the floor to get you back for being so busy, or did your apparent withholding of affection cause him so much stress that he lost control?

If you know what your dog expects and what causes him distress, then you will be less likely to yell at him for things he didn't do "on purpose." Yelling, or even worse, hitting your dog is extremely confusing and damaging to your relationship. He'll have an image of you yelling or doling out pain, but he won't be clear why. Seemingly random, frightening behavior from you will eventually erode your relationship with your dog. He'll lose trust in you, you'll think he's untrainable, and boom . . . one more dog abandoned to the animal shelter, where chances are slim that he'll be readopted.

Can't We All Just Get Along?

Thinking like a dog can indeed help you and your dog to get along, agree on some house rules and mutually beneficial behavior, and maintain a lifelong fulfilling relationship. First, don't set your dog up to fail. Don't leave things around that he will tend to destroy. Give him things with your smell on them that he is allowed to chew—but not shoes, because then he'll think shoes are okay for chewing. Pay attention to your dog and what his habits and tendencies are so that you can redirect his behavior when necessary. You can't just ignore your dog and expect him to know how to behave.

You can also make imagery work for you. If you know your dog gets overly emotional when you leave, make it a habit *not* to make a big deal before leaving or when coming home so that your transition times are calm rather than dramatic. Socialize your dog by giving him lots of positive images associated with all kinds of people, animals, and situations. Save the negative imagery for direct links to behavior you don't like, such as a very quick sharp "No!" if he tries to bolt out the front door. Don't yell at him when he comes back after running out the door, or he'll think you are angry at him for coming back.

Later in this book you'll get more specific directions on training, but for now, just keep in mind that your dog probably thinks in images and in terms of positive and negative associations with those images, and you'll be on your way to better communication and a firm foundation for a strong human–canine relationship.

Think, But Don't Act, Like a Dog

The last key to your dog's mind to keep in *your* mind is that while you will benefit from knowing how your dog thinks, you won't benefit from acting like your dog. Some books tell you to behave like a member of the pack, but that this is the worst thing a human can do, because dogs are faster and have sharper teeth. If your dog thinks you are just another dog, he may try to challenge you. However, if he thinks you are some kind of super dog, with the amazing talent to walk on two legs and make all kinds of fascinating vocal inflections, expressions, and movements, if he thinks that he could never ever be as amazing and powerful as you, then he'll feel safe and confident that you are in control. He won't have to be.

The trick is to act like an assertive but kind *human being*, one who understands dogs—their motivations, their desires, their fears, and their needs—but is bigger and better and smarter than a dog.

You can do that.

Dogs take the lead from people they admire.

PART TWO

A HEALTHY

FOUNDATION

3

FEEDING FOR GOOD HEALTH

Dogs eat dog food. That sounds simple enough, but actually the type of food, how much is fed, and the manner in which it is fed to your dog can all have a drastic impact on your pet's health and longevity. As your dog's guardian, it is your job to make sure he gets the right amount of protein, vitamins, minerals, fats, and calories to stay fit and healthy. Obesity is a common problem among pet dogs, but even dogs at a healthy weight may not be getting optimum nutrition, because the foods they eat don't provide them with enough absorbable protein for their needs, enough fat for their coats, or the right carbohydrates to facilitate energy and digestion.

This chapter will help you to determine exactly what your dog needs and what his food should contain. If you've never peeked at that dog food label before, it's time to drag out that bag of kibble or that can of meaty chunks and take a good hard look. Keep that label with you as you read this chapter. You'll want to refer to it often.

YOUR DOG'S DIETARY NEEDS

Humans are omnivorous, meaning we can survive on many types of food, from plant foods to animal foods. In fact, the only food humans don't seem to thrive on is overly processed food. But what about dogs?

Welcome to the latest great debate. Some authorities believe that dogs

Dogs Love Treats

Everybody loves treats, and your dog is no exception, but a treat doesn't have to come from a pet store. You can find healthy additions to your dog's diet right in your own refrigerator . . . in the produce bin! Avoid fattening treats to keep your dog in optimal health. Instead, see how many of the following nonfat, high-fiber, nutrient-packed goodies your dog enjoys (limit to two per day for small dogs to ensure they don't fill up and shun their regular balanced diet):

- blueberries
- broccoli florets
- green beans, cooked or raw
- peas
- raw baby carrots

are carnivorous since wolves are carnivorous. Dogs and wolves have similar sharp fangs for tearing meat and do not produce amylase, the enzyme common to herbivores and omnivores that digests carbohydrates during chewing, in their saliva. Others argue that even wolves are known to graze on plants and eat the herbaceous stomach contents of their prey and that the domestic dog's long evolution as a scavenger has resulted in an omnivorous animal who can survive on just about any food it can find.

It's true that many dogs thrive on carbohydrates. Although it's also true that most dogs seem to do best on a balanced diet that contains a large amount of meat, there are anecdotal stories about dogs surviving or even thriving on many kinds of diets, but one could say the same thing about humans. It may be that the ideal human and canine eating patterns really aren't so different after all. Dogs may or may not need more meat than humans, but we are both likely on the omnivorous spectrum and do best on high-quality whole foods rather than processed foods.

The bottom line is that dogs need fiber, carbohydrates, and fats from plant foods, as well as the vitamins and minerals plants contain. Most veterinarians agree, however, that the primary source of protein in a dog's diet should be meat, and the first (ideally, the first two or even three) ingredients on your dog's food bag should come from meat. A food that lists cornmeal, rice, barley, or some other grain, or another starch like potato, as the first ingredient may not have the available protein a meat-based food will have. A carbohydrate source like corn, rice, barley, or potato as a third or fourth ingredient is fine, however, and provides your

Dogs were born for eating meat, but they also need nutrients from plant foods.

dog with fiber, vitamins, minerals, and fatty acids from vegetable oil. Whole grains and root vegetables are probably superior nutritionally to processed grains.

Digestibility

Another thing to consider is the source of protein in the food you choose for your dog. Some proteins are more digestible than others. Proteins from muscle meat are highly digestible. Grains contain some protein but less protein than animal products, and their protein is also

less digestible for dogs. Proteins from animal by-products (parts from animals that are not smooth muscle tissue) may or may not be as digestible as muscle meat, depending on the quality of the by-products and what they are—something the food bag likely won't tell you.

What the food bag will tell you, however, is the percentage of protein in the food. But just because a dog food contains a certain percentage of protein doesn't mean your dog will actually use that much protein, and while some dog foods boast digestibility statistics (82 to 86 percent digestibility is about as high as is possible for high-quality protein), that information is not required by law. Neither are the contents of a "by-product" or "by-product meal" or even "meat meal." In other words, the dog food label is informative, but it may not tell you everything you really want to know.

How do you know how digestible your dog's food is? Look for a food that lists regular meat or meat meal as the first ingredient, and meat, meat meal, meat by-products, or meat by-product meal as the second and even the third ingredient. If the third or fourth ingredient is a grain, you probably have a food with high digestibility. Higher-priced "premium" or "super-premium" foods are more likely to contain

Some foods are more digestible than others. Dogs only benefit from protein they can digest.

higher-quality and more digestible proteins than "economy" foods, but this isn't always true. It's always a good idea to read the label. A few of the more expensive brands do list grains as the first ingredients and may also include other undesirable ingredients, like a lot of chemical preservatives and even sugar. Best to stick with those that list meat first and at least one other meat source second or third.

Beyond Protein

Dogs need more than protein. They need fat and carbohydrates for energy. While dogs (and people) can use protein for energy in a pinch, fats and carbs are more efficient energy

sources and allow for the body to use protein to build and repair itself.

Dogs can manufacture most fatty acids on their own except for linoleic acid (omega-6), which they must ingest. Linoleic acid is important for keeping your dog healthy because it keeps his skin, nose, paw pads, and coat soft, pliable, and shiny. Meats and grain oils contain linoleic acid.

Carbohydrates supply cells with glucose, which not only supplies the body with energy but also helps digestion and keeps muscles and the brain in good working order. Simple carbohydrates make for quick energy. These come from grains like corn, rice, barley, and oatmeal as well as other starches like potatoes, sweet potatoes, and taro root. Complex carbohydrates like cellulose are a good source of fiber, which regulates water in your dog's large intestine and keeps your dog's bowels moving efficiently. Dog foods may contain other sources of fiber, too.

Dogs require 14 vitamins: thiamin (B1), riboflavin (B2), pantothenic acid (B5), pyridoxine (B6), niacin, vitamin B12, folic acid, biotin, choline, vitamin C, vitamin A, vitamin D, vitamin E, and vitamin K. They also require the minerals calcium, phosphorus, magnesium, sulfur, iron, copper, zinc, manganese, iodine, selenium, and cobalt.

The vitamin and mineral balance your dog requires is tough to figure out on your own, so relying on a complete fortified dog food may be the best way to keep your dog's diet nutritionally sound. If you make your own dog food, you'll need to make sure these vitamins and minerals are present in the proper proportions. If you feed a quality dog food, that balance should already be in place.

ALL ABOUT DOG FOOD

Let's look at that dog food label again. You'll see lots of different things listed there, and you probably don't know what they all are. Manufacturers are required to list ingredients by dry-weight amount, meaning the most prevalent

Complete fortified dog foods can provide the right balance of vitamins and minerals.

ingredient is listed first. However, if a grain is broken down into parts, such as ground corn and corn gluten meal or wheat flour, wheat germ meal, and wheat bran, then it can look like a food is mostly meat-based when actually the grains are the primary ingredient. Another way to make a dog food look like it contains more meat than it really does is to include many different grains in a dog food, like ground corn, rice flour, wheat flour, and soy flour. These might all be listed as the third, fourth, sixth, and seventh ingredients but could result in a grain-based food disguised as a meat-based food.

A basic and sensible rule of thumb when surveying an ingredients list is to choose a food with more quality

ingredients you recognize in the least processed forms: meat over meat meal; meat meal over by-product meal; ground grains over grain meal; vegetables over vegetable parts; etc.

Also avoid foods with artificial colorings and flavorings and added sugar and/or corn syrup.

Now let's look at the different forms dog food can take.

Dry Kibble

A dry kibble helps to clean your dog's teeth, and high-quality dry kibbles contain digestible proteins and all the vitamins, minerals, fats, and carbohydrates your dog requires. A good dry kibble can be an excellent source of nutrition. Kibble is cheaper than canned food (even the premium brands), and your dog doesn't have to eat as much kibble as canned food to get the same nutrition. Kibble won't spoil in your pet's food bowl if it sits there all day.

Some dry kibble is very economical but less nutritious. Dogs on economy kibble may suffer from poor coats, skin problems, large stool volume (not fun to pick up), and other health problems, especially in sensitive or allergic dogs.

Kibbles labeled "premium" or "super-premium" usually contain higher-quality ingredients but not necessarily in ideal proportions. "Natural" foods may contain more natural preservatives or other extra ingredients like herbs, digestive aids, or organic ingredients. Read the label.

Your Dog's Daily Multivitamin?

Because high-quality dog foods are typically subject to feeding trials (it should say so on the bag), they have been carefully formulated to contain just the right balance of vitamins and minerals. If you also give your dog vitamin and/or mineral supplements, you can throw off this balance, which could cause health problems for your dog. Unless you are feeding a homemade diet or your dog has a special nutritional need so that your vet recommends supplementation, leave the vitamin and mineral supplementation to the experts.

No law governs the use of these terms, so it's buyer beware.

Despite the high-quality nature of many dry dog foods, some people don't like the highly processed nature of kibble. The ingredients in dry kibble are often rendered into meal (processed to remove all fats and oils), and then the dog food mix is processed further by going through an extruder, which mixes, heats, and then cuts and dries the kibble. Extrusion processes dog food at such a high heat that some of the proteins and vitamins are broken down and lost. Natural enzymes in the food are also destroyed. Vitamins must then be sprayed back onto

the food along with fat and flavoring to make the kibble taste good. It's a far cry from catching and eating a rabbit, chewing on a bone, or munching on grass.

Semi-Moist Food

Semi-moist foods aren't extruded, so they contain more water. They also contain a lot more preservatives, colorings, and sugar to make them safe and palatable and to prevent spoilage. These added ingredients make them poor choices for good nutrition, even if your dog likes his little bone-shaped, chewy bits better than dry kibble.

Canned Food

Canned dog food contains high amounts of water. It is more expensive than dry food, and because it isn't hard, it doesn't help to clean your dog's teeth. In fact, it may even lead to tooth decay because it is more likely to stick to teeth. If you feed your dog canned food, be sure to brush his teeth regularly.

Canned food, once opened, doesn't last long and will spoil if your dog doesn't eat it right away. He may have to eat more canned food to get the same nutrition, which can get pretty pricey, especially for large dogs.

Because canned food isn't extruded, it may contain more intact proteins, vitamins, and enzymes than dry kibble, and some dogs prefer the taste. However, canned food may not be quite as meaty as it appears—many canned foods, especially cheaper ones, contain a lot of wheat gluten, which has a similar texture to meat but is less digestible than animal protein. If you choose a canned food, make sure it is approved by AAFCO as a complete diet and contains quality ingredients, including fresh meat as the first two ingredients, and make sure you keep your dog's teeth clean with a dental treat and regular brushing. (You'll learn more about dental health later in this book.)

Also, because canned food contains more water, percentages of protein, fat, and carbohydrates

Semi-moist foods contain more preservatives, colorings, and sugar than other dog foods.

can't be compared with dry foods. On a dry-weight basis, canned foods actually contain more protein than dry kibble, even though it doesn't look that way on the label. Instead, compare canned foods with other canned foods to find the best nutrient profile.

Custom Formulas

Some dog foods are custom-made for dogs with certain problems or certain traits. Some lines make foods specifically formulated for small, medium, large, and giant dogs because differently sized dogs have different nutritional needs. For example, very large dogs need lower protein and calcium so that they don't grow too quickly, compromising their bone density. Fast

If you feed your dog canned food, be sure to brush his teeth regularly.

Some foods are custom-made for dogs with certain ailments, lifestyles, or traits.

growth in giant breeds (like Great Danes) can lead to orthopedic problems later in life. Very small dogs, on the other hand, require more frequent meals with plenty of energy, especially if they are active. Toy dog formulas are typically more nutrient dense.

Some dog foods are made for different types of dogs. Performance dog foods have higher protein, fat, and calories for hardworking hunting dogs, working dogs (such as police or search-and-rescue dogs), and dog athletes (such as those participating in agility, flyball, or weight-pulling competitions). Senior formulas are for older dogs at risk for certain diseases of aging or who may now be less active. Weight-loss formulas typically contain less fat and more fiber, to keep dogs full on fewer calories.

Still others are formulated for dogs with specific health problems, such as arthritis, heart disease, kidney problems, allergies, or dental issues. Ask your vet if a custom dog food formula might be best for your dog, and don't forget to read the label. Just because it's custom-made doesn't necessarily mean it's better. Some prescription foods contain corn as the first ingredient, when a more digestible protein source might be preferable. If you have questions about the ingredients in your dog's prescription food, ask your veterinarian.

HOW MUCH, HOW OFTEN?

People often wonder if they are feeding their overweight dogs too much, even though they are following the instructions on the kibble bag. While dog food does include guidelines showing you how much to feed dogs of different weights, these are guidelines only. If your dog is overweight, he is probably eating too much and exercising too little.

Most dogs simply eat too much, but every dog is different. Some dogs eat a lot and stay thin and fit, usually because they are active (or high-strung!). Other dogs hardly ever exercise and remain slim, often because it is a breed characteristic. On the other hand, some highly active dogs sport a prodigious girth. More commonly, however, pets are overweight. In fact, veterinarians agree that excessive weight is the most common chronic health issue for pet dogs, and this is almost always due to overeating.

The best way to tell if you are feeding the right amount is to look at your dog. Does he have a nice tuck below his ribs indicating a waistline? If so, he is probably in good shape. If he has no

What's in the Food?

Ingredient	What It Is
Meat	Clean muscle meat from cattle, swine, sheep (or lambs), or goats, including muscle, tongue, heart, esophagus, and diaphragm.
Poultry	Clean muscle meat (as above) from chicken or turkey.
By-products	Non-rendered protein from animal carcasses not approved for human consumption, not including meat but including organs, blood, bones, fat, and intestines, and in the case of poultry, heads, feet, and undeveloped eggs. It may not contain hair, feathers, horns, beaks, teeth, or hoofs.
Meat or poultry meal	Rendered (fat-removed) meal made from animal parts, containing no more than 14 percent indigestible materials. Meat meal cannot contain hair, feathers, horns, beaks, teeth, hooves, blood, skin, feces, or intestinal contents. Meat meal comes from cattle, swine, sheep, lamb, or goats. Poultry meal comes from chicken or turkeys. Meat and bone meal may also contain rendered bone.
Animal by-product meal	Rendered (fat-removed) by-products (as described above).

How Much?

Wouldn't it be nice if you could plug your dog's weight into a formula and get the exact amount of food for the perfect diet? Unfortunately, it's not that simple. The amount of food your dog needs depends on several things, like the nutrient density of the food and your dog's activity level, age, and metabolism. For example, premium and super-premium foods are more nutrient dense than economy foods, so your dog doesn't need as much. This makes a higher-quality food a pretty good deal, economically, even with the higher price tag. Canned food also differs in amount, so consult the directions, which typically provide a range depending on your dog's weight.

Always start by feeding your dog on the low end of the dog food's suggested guidelines. For example, a dry kibble might recommend 3/4 to 1 1/4 cups (177–296 mL) per day for a 15-pound (7-kg) dog. Start with that

You can check your fluffy or shaggy dog's weight by feeling his ribs.

visible waistline and appears sausage-shaped, he is probably overweight. If that waist tuck is so extreme as to appear emaciated, he may not be getting enough food.

Another test is to feel your dog's ribs. Because dogs have different coats, you can't always tell by looking. You should be able to slightly make out the lines of the ribs in smooth-coated dogs like Greyhounds and Dobermans. In shaggier dogs, you'll have to feel your dog's ribs. Can you feel them? If so, great! If they are imperceptible, your dog may be overweight.

Keep Moving

Don't forget that just as with humans, exercise is important for preventing or reversing obesity in pets. Get that dog of yours moving every day—if not on a walk, then at least for a romp around the yard.

3/4 cup (177 mL), especially if your dog gets treats or occasional healthy people food as a supplement (or if he hangs around under your kids at the dining room table). Unless he is highly active, the low-end requirement is probably plenty. If your dog is always hungry and looks too thin, up the amount a bit. (If he is always hungry and overweight, don't give in to those pleading eyes, but do see your vet if you suspect a health problem.) Also remember that the amount on the bag is *per day,* not per meal, so if you feed your dog more than once a day (which is a good idea for most dogs, who can benefit from spreading their energy intake out over the day), divide the amount by the number of feedings.

If you are unsure about whether your dog is overweight or underweight, ask your vet to help you determine your dog's status and a healthy diet and exercise plan.

How Often?

While many people feed their dogs only once a day, most people like to eat more often than that. Most dogs probably prefer it, too.

Start by feeding your dog on the low end of his food's suggested guidelines.

Small dogs and especially puppies must eat more than once a day because they have small stomachs and quick metabolisms. Those little bits of food are digested quickly and waiting another 24 hours for a meal can be hard on your tiny pup.

Consult your vet if the following guidelines don't work for you because, of course, every dog is different, but for most dogs, a feeding schedule that works well might go something like this:

- 8 weeks to 12 weeks: 4 times per day
- 12 weeks to 6 months: 3 times per day
- 6 months through adulthood for dogs under 15 pounds (7 kg): 3 times per day
- 6 months through adulthood for dogs over 15 pounds (7 kg): 2 times per day

HOMEMADE DIETS

Some people just feel better about making their own dog food. This is a controversial subject, however. Dog food companies and many vets warn against a home-prepared diet because it could lack nutrients dogs need, resulting in deficiencies and health issues. Many pet owners, dog breeders, and more holistically oriented veterinarians, however, think that a home-prepared diet is ideal for dogs, especially those with many allergies or food sensitivities.

If you like the idea, love to cook, and choose a whole-food diet for yourself, you might be a good candidate to try this method of feeding your dog. Cooking for your dog can be fun, and a high-quality homemade diet may provide your dog with noticeable health benefits. However, if you

Homemade diets should provide your dog with all the nutrients he requires in the right proportions.

When Food = Poison

You may have heard that dogs have strong stomachs and can digest just about everything, but some foods are very dangerous for dogs, and some dogs are more sensitive to these foods than others. For his health, please don't let your dog eat any of the foods on this list:

- alcohol
- avocado pits and skin
- chocolate
- coffee and tea
- cooked bones
- dairy products
- fruit pits
- grapes and raisins

- macadamia nuts
- onions
- mold
- rotten or spoiled food
- salt
- xylitol (the sweetener common in sugar-free gum and toothpaste)
- yeast dough

choose to make your own dog food, you must be vigilant.

Even though dog food is a relatively recent invention—James Spratt marketed the first commercially prepared dog food around 1860, while earlier pets got by on leftover table scraps—there are no studies to show how many dogs from before the days of Spratt's Patent Meat Fibrine Dog Cakes suffered from nutritional deficiencies. Also, remember that our 19th-century ancestors tended to eat a much healthier, less processed diet of fresh meat, grains, and vegetables. Leftovers from our 21st-century dining tables (or fast food bags and take-out containers) aren't as healthy for our pets. Still, you may think to yourself: *I don't have a formulated kibble. I eat what I want and I do just fine.*

This is a fair argument, but at the same time, many veterinarians report seeing dogs with serious health issues related to nutritional deficiencies due to well-meant but ill-prepared home cooking.

The trick is to provide your dog with all the protein, fat, carbohydrates, vitamins, and minerals he requires in just the right proportions. Yes, dog food companies do that work for us. But plenty of people like to do it on their own. Do a little research and you should be able to fare just as well as, if not a whole lot better than, a dog food company.

However, telling you how to prepare a nutritionally complete home-prepared canine diet is beyond the scope of this book. There are excellent books that go into great detail about all that is involved and all the options you have when it comes to cooking for your own dog. Look online, or ask your veterinarian for suggestions, if she is open to the idea. You can also consult your dog's breeder (or the shelter where you adopted your dog) or talk to dog-savvy friends. A simple online search will reveal many options in varying degrees of difficulty.

Feed the Itch

When dogs get allergic reactions, they tend to itch, and when dogs itch but don't have fleas, people tend to assume they have food allergies. Actually, about 90 percent of allergic reactions in dogs are to environmental triggers like pollen. Only about 10 percent of allergies are due to a food. Even then, one of the most common food allergens for dogs is wheat, but although many people assume the grains are to blame (gluten intolerance being a hot topic in human nutrition), more often the culprit is a meat protein, like beef, chicken, lamb, or fish, or another protein, like eggs or soy. Some dogs are allergic to the protein in wheat, and a dog with food allergies is also likely to have multiple food allergies, but treat your dog for environmental allergies first. If that doesn't work, your veterinarian can help you determine the best way to pin down a food allergy.

Raw Versus Cooked

Many proponents of homemade diets strongly recommend using raw meat rather than cooked in homemade dog food recipes. Raw meat contains more enzymes and, although it also contains bacteria, some believe the dog's strong digestive acids easily conquer bacteria, and in the process, the dog's immune system grows stronger. The raw meat diet also has its detractors. Not only do some people dislike handling raw meat, but the bacteria factor makes them nervous, and rightly so. Young children, the elderly, and those with compromised immune systems should never handle raw meat.

Another good option, if you believe in raw feeding, is commercially prepared raw food. Some companies have done all the work for you, mixing up and freezing raw food in patties or pellets. You just take the appropriate amount out of the freezer the night before, let it thaw, and feed it to your dog the next day. You might not ever need to touch it.

Talk to your vet or your dog's breeder about which method might work best, consider your personal situation and family members, and do your own research. Only you can decide what will work best for your dog.

The Complete Nutritional Picture

If you feed your dog a homemade diet, you are responsible for making sure he gets everything he needs.

This takes some research and a long-term commitment, as I've already explained. However, there is a pretty good way to be sure your homemade diet is keeping your dog on track for good health.

Before you change your dog's diet, have your veterinarian do a blood panel to determine the basic parameters of your dog's health. After you start your homemade diet regimen, repeat the test every few months. If the numbers remain steady, or even improve, this can reassure you (and your vet) that you are feeding your dog in a nutritionally sound manner.

Here's the bottom line: If you are willing to have these tests done, willing to learn what you must know to give your dog everything he needs, and willing to mix up all the necessary ingredients for your dog often enough to provide him with good fresh food every day, then a homemade diet might be a good option for you. However, if this is too much of a commitment (as it is for most of us), you are better off feeding your dog a high-quality commercially prepared food.

Raw diets can be nutritious, but they are also potentially hazardous.

4

GROOMING FOR GOOD HEALTH

G rooming can bring out the best in your dog: the glorious white curls of a Poodle; the gleaming ebony sheen of a Doberman; the magnificent red mane of a Pekingese; the tawny, flowing silk of a Yorkshire Terrier; the feathery ruff of a foxy Pomeranian—I could go on and on! Good grooming certainly helps your dog look beautiful, but grooming is more than just cosmetic. Grooming is an essential component to good health.

Whether your dog has a short, hard coat like a Beagle, a medium coat like a Golden Retriever, a long, showy coat like a Shih Tzu, or a coat full of curls like a Poodle or a Puli, that coat needs grooming. The skin beneath the coat needs care and attention too, as do your dog's nails, paw pads, ears, eyes, and teeth. Grooming means more than brushing out a dog once a week and sending him on his merry way. Grooming is all about sound personal canine hygiene, and because your dog can't bathe himself, trim his own nails, brush his teeth, or treat his own skin allergies, the job falls to you.

Grooming your dog is all about sound personal canine hygiene.

WEEKLY GROOMING: A HEALTHY RITUAL

Some dogs barely need a brush and always look immaculate, while others get matted when 24 hours pass without comb to coat. But even dogs who don't necessarily need weekly grooming can benefit from it for other reasons. In most cases (except for heavily coated breeds prone to matting, who need more frequent brushing), a once-a-week grooming session is a great habit for any dog–human team to cultivate.

Weekly grooming sessions give you and your dog a great opportunity to bond, and they give you the chance to check your dog over. If you give your dog an "exam" at the start of each session, you will be more likely to catch any health problems evident on his skin or coat before they get too serious. A grooming exam also accustoms your dog to the kind of handling he will get from a vet, making visits easier for everyone.

You can adapt the following steps for you and your dog. For instance, brushing is listed as the final step here, but if your dog is in serious need of coat care and the coat is impeding access to nails, ears, and eyes, do the coat first. In general, a weekly grooming session should include the following:

First, call your dog to come to a certain spot you always use for

Grooming Must-Haves

Every dog owner should have the following grooming supplies handy. Keeping them in a basket or tackle box in the spot where you will groom your dog makes everything easy to find:

- blow dryer with low-heat or cool setting for dogs with long, curly, or fluffy coats
- brushes and combs appropriate for your dog's coat
- conditioner and/or coat-conditioning spray appropriate for your dog's coat
- guillotine- or scissors-style nail trimmers made for your dog's size (don't use human nail trimmers on dogs)
- shampoo appropriate for your dog's coat or all-purpose, high-quality dog shampoo
- small haircutting or nail scissors (depending on the size of your dog) for trimming excess hair from around toes and paw pads, ears, and eyes, and for clipping extra-long whiskers and neatening stray hairs around the coat
- styptic pencil or other antiseptic coagulant to stop bleeding if you accidentally trim the nail's quick
- toothbrush made for dogs
- toothpaste made for dogs

grooming: the back porch, the bathroom, the family room, or wherever is comfortable, where you can easily reach your dog, and which can be easily cleaned afterward. For small dogs, a counter or table with a non-slip surface is helpful. Even a card table topped with a rubber mat will do the trick, or if you want to go all the way, invest in a grooming table, which stands at just the right height.

Skin Rubdown

Start by giving your dog a rubdown all over his skin, like a massage. Rub head to toe, which will help loosen dead hairs in the coat. Your dog will enjoy it, and if he has any lumps, bumps, dry skin patches, or sore areas, you'll find them. (If you do encounter any problems, call your vet to have them checked out.)

Next, pick up each of your dog's feet. Press on his paw pads and wiggle his toes. Doing this from puppyhood will make toenail clipping much easier when your dog is big and strong. Don't clip toenails just yet, though, so your dog doesn't associate every foot handling with toenail clipping.

Weekly grooming sessions give you the chance to bond with and check up on your dog.

Ear Exam

Examine your dog's ears. Lift them up if they hang over. Look inside. Rub them and check for lumps. If they are dirty, clean them out with a cotton ball and mineral oil or special ear cleaner made for dogs. Don't stick anything way down inside a dog's ear, but clean as far as you can see. Dogs with long, floppy ears are particularly prone to yeast infections, and pests like fleas and ticks are often visible on the ears, so take a good close look. After cleaning, make sure your dog's ears are thoroughly dry, as moisture can also promote yeast or bacterial infections.

Eye Inspection

Examine your dog's eyes and wipe away any discharge. If your dog has a white coat and tearstains, you can use a special product made to remove tearstains (usually a cosmetic problem only). Check for irritation, too. Some dogs suffer from entropion, a genetic condition in which the lid turns inward and eyelashes can scratch your dog's cornea. Also check that the eyes are clear. Cloudiness could indicate cataracts, so see your vet if you think your dog's eyes look cloudy. Redness and irritation can also indicate a foreign object in the eye. Don't try to remove anything from your dog's eye yourself. See your vet. If your dog has allergies, his eyes could become red and irritated. See your vet if you suspect seasonal allergies.

Those Droopy Eyes

Scenthounds who spend a lot of time with their noses to the ground can be prone to getting foreign objects in their eyes, especially if they spend their days trailing or just snuffling around outside in heavy brush. Bloodhounds in particular have quite a few folds and droops around the eyes and a lower lid that pulls up to protect the eyes against underbrush. Any dog with lots of facial skin folds needs a little extra attention to the eye area. Moisture and dirt can collect within skin folds of the eye and become infected. Keep skin folds around the eyes clean and dry by wiping them down at least once a week with a damp, soft cloth and drying them thoroughly.

Tooth Check

Next, pull back your dog's lips and get a good look at his teeth. Are they white and shiny, or yellow with plaque? Oral bacteria has been linked to heart disease in dogs, so keeping your dog's teeth clean and plaque-free is essential for good health, especially in senior dogs. Make sure your dog gets to eat something crunchy every day—dental treats are made for this purpose, but crunchy biscuits made with high-quality ingredients or raw veggies or fruit (like baby carrots, broccoli florets,

can make nail trimming much easier. See a groomer or your vet to have a very resistant dog's nails trimmed, but the job will be much easier and cheaper if you can do it yourself. First, take a look at your dog's nails. If they are light colored, you can see the quick, a vein that runs about halfway down the nail. Dark nails will hide the quick. Begin by snipping off just the tip of your dog's nails with the guillotine- or scissors-style nail trimmer. You could also grind them flat with a Dremel tool or nail grinder, but be careful not to grind the nail down too far, and avoid these if your dog has long paw hair that could get caught by the rotating parts. If you trim your dog's nails every week, they will stay short. If you've waited awhile, you may have to cut off more.

At last, you are ready to manage that lovely coat. The tools and techniques to use depend on your dog's coat type, so read on to determine the best way to groom your dog's crowning glory.

and apple slices) are good, too. Also invest in a toothbrush or tooth scrubber (these fit over your finger) and toothpaste made just for dogs. Dogs can get sick from eating human toothpaste, but dog toothpaste is edible and tastes like meat, so dogs can't resist it. Brush your dog's teeth carefully and remember how important it is that your dog accepts handling of his mouth by you, your vet, and any prospective show dog judges, too.

Nail Trim

Time to clip those nails! Some dogs dislike nail trimming, but handling a dog's feet every day from puppyhood

Coat Care

Who needs a bath? Maybe your dog does . . . and maybe he doesn't. Some dogs, such as certain scenthounds and those with long coats who spend a lot of time working hard outdoors and getting really dirty, tend to develop odors due to lots of sebaceous glands and/or skin folds. Dirt and moisture left unwashed can also attract bacteria and encourage matting, and could even result in skin infection. These dogs can benefit from baths as often as daily, but weekly or even every other week might be fine. Or bathe your dog after particularly dirty outdoor sessions or when you notice an odor.

Other dogs, such as those with smooth coats and sensitive skin, don't need a bath more than a couple of times a year unless they have an encounter with something stinky, sticky, or extra dirty. Excessive bathing might even cause more skin problems than it prevents, especially if you aren't using a very mild, hypoallergenic canine shampoo.

But no matter whether you do it often or not often at all, every pet owner should know how to give her pup a bath.

First, decide where you will bathe your dog. The bathtub works for most dogs, but close the doors and have plenty of towels ready so that your sopping wet pup doesn't escape and go bounding around the house spraying water. Some larger dogs may enjoy an outdoor bath with the garden hose and a big

> Check your dog's ears, eyes, coat, and mouth during each grooming session.

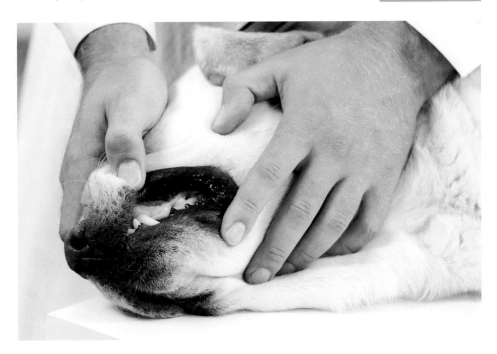

tub or kiddie pool, but make sure the hose water hasn't been sitting in the sun. In other words, don't burn your dog! Test the water first, and never bathe a dog outside if the weather is even a little bit chilly.

Brush and comb out your dog's coat, removing all tangles and mats. If your dog has mats you can't remove, have a groomer try, unless you prefer to clip your dog's coat short. (This can compromise a show coat's quality, so be sure that's what you really want to do.)

Once the coat is tangle-free, soak your dog thoroughly with lukewarm water to the skin. A handheld showerhead works well. Apply dog shampoo appropriate for your dog's coat and work through with a sponge or your fingers. Brush the shampoo into your dog's coat with a bristle brush. Use a small bristle brush around the face to avoid getting shampoo in the eyes. Rinse your dog thoroughly to the skin to remove all the shampoo. Apply conditioner according to the directions and rinse again. Squeeze excess water from your dog's coat with your hands and towel dry thoroughly.

Blow-dry long coats and thick or double short coats on a low setting while brushing with a bristle brush.

All pet owners should know how to give their dogs a bath.

Short, wiry, and smooth coats can air-dry. Long coats can get puffy without blow-drying and brushing, which gives them a smooth texture. Blow-dry curly coats according to how you want them to look when dry—talk to your groomer.

Unless you want your wet puppy rolling around joyfully in the mud, keep him inside until he is completely dry.

COAT TYPES

Dogs may all be members of *Canis familiaris*, but when it comes to coats, they are about as different as you can imagine. Put a black and tan Manchester Terrier next to a black Miniature Poodle in a full show clip and the difference is clear. Your dog's coat type determines the necessary grooming tools and techniques, and coats come in six basic types:

1. Longhaired coats, like those of the Shih Tzu, Bearded Collie, English Toy Spaniel, and Afghan Hound. These dogs have very long coats, sometimes woolly and sometimes silky.
2. Shorthaired coats, like those of the Labrador Retriever, Rottweiler, German Shepherd, and Pembroke Welsh Corgi. Some people lump shorthaired coats and smooth coats together, but shorthaired coats can be considered separately, as they are thicker and fuller than smooth coats but still on the short side.
3. Medium coats, like those of the Golden Retriever, Akita, Brittany, and Border Collie. These dogs have longer hair, sometimes silky, sometimes feathered, but are still relatively easy to groom.
4. Smooth coats, like those of the Boxer, Beagle, Great Dane, and Whippet. These dogs have sleek, shiny, thin coats.

Don't Clip That Quick!

The more you trim your dog's nails, the farther back the quick will recede, but if you accidentally clip the quick—the vein that runs partway down your dog's nail—your dog's nail will bleed. Apply a styptic pencil or other antiseptic coagulant to the nail. Clipping the quick hurts and your dog won't like it. He might yelp or pull away if he is very sensitive, so avoid this if possible. However, a clipped quick is not an emergency, even if you don't have a way to stop the bleeding. It will coagulate on its own eventually. Stopping the bleeding is mostly for the benefit of your carpets and furniture. If this happens to you, stay calm, reassure your dog without making a big deal of it, and move on to the next step. If you continue to trim the nails every week without incident, your dog should soon learn that nail clipping doesn't have to be painful or startling and is just one more part of the regular routine.

5. Wirehaired or broken coats, like those of the Schnauzer, Westie, Airedale Terrier, and Cairn Terrier. These dogs have stiff, wiry coats.
6. Curly coats, like those of the Poodle, Puli, Irish Water Spaniel, and Bedlington Terrier. These dogs have bouncy curls, cool cords, or sculptable frizz, depending on how they are groomed.

Let's look at each type and what is required to keep that special coat at its most beautiful.

Longhaired Coats

Whether you've got a tiny Maltese or a magnificent Afghan Hound, if you have to groom a longhaired coat, you have some serious work to do. You will probably spend far more time brushing out your dog than anyone whose dog has a different coat type. Let a longhaired coat go unbrushed for more than a week, and you have an even more prodigious job. A badly matted long coat may indeed be beyond saving, and your only option may be to shave the dog and start over. For this reason, regular brushing at least *every other day* is essential for longhaired breeds, and a thorough down-to-the-skin brush and comb-out should be a weekly habit.

Because brushing and combing a longhaired breed

Your dog's coat type determines the necessary grooming tools and techniques.

takes so long, it can become an excellent way for you and your pet to spend time together. Brush and comb your little Lhasa Apso or Tibetan Terrier in front of the TV each evening or after the morning walk. Longhaired breeds trained from puppyhood to stand patiently for brushing will be much easier to keep well-groomed.

Many owners of dogs with longhaired coats choose to have their pets professionally groomed about once a month because they don't have the time to keep those long lovely coats in perfect condition, but even so, longhaired breeds require regular brushing sessions to maintain the coat between professional groomings.

Others opt to keep their longhaired friends in so-called "puppy clips" or "pet clips" or other shorter styles like Schnauzer trims to make those long coats more practical and easier to manage, not to mention less prone to matting. If you have a longhaired breed because you love that gorgeous coat, you may find the extra work worth it, but if you just love your little puppy because of his sparkling personality, you may really enjoy the convenience of a pet clip.

Mats are not only unsightly. They can hide skin conditions and other problems on a dog, so keep your longhaired friend in good coat. The

great thing about brushing a longhaired breed is the end result. A freshly brushed Shih Tzu, Yorkie, Pomeranian, or Chow Chow is a glorious sight and well worth the effort.

Longhaired coats require far more brushing than other coat types.

Other longhaired breeds, such as Samoyeds, Collies, and sheepdogs, are also sometimes shaved down when they get overly matted or with the change of seasons. These larger breeds take even longer to brush out but are spectacular in their full coats.

Grooming the Longhaired Coat
Brushing a longhaired coat is different from brushing any other kind of coat. If

the job looks too tough, consult a professional, but for daily brushing and grooming, follow these steps:

- Spray coat with coat conditioner to make brushing easier and less damaging to hair.
- Brush through with pin brush, or in the case of a neglected coat, a wire slicker brush.
- For heavy coats, brush in layers.
- For the Lhasa Apso, Shih Tzu, Yorkshire Terrier, Silky Terrier, Skye Terrier, Tibetan Terrier, Maltese, and Afghan Hound, make a straight part with a comb down the back and brush coat down on either side.
- Comb through mats with mat comb.

Longhaired Coat Grooming Tools

- basic comb with coarse (widely spaced teeth) and fine (narrowly spaced teeth) sides
- blow dryer with low setting
- conditioner for long coats
- large bristle brush
- mat comb
- pin brush
- shampoo for long coats
- small bristle brush
- small scissors
- spray coat conditioner
- wire slicker brush

- Comb hair with coarse side of basic comb.
- Comb hair with fine side of basic comb.

Shampoo your longhaired dog at least once every month.

- Trim excess hair from around the feet, so hair is level with the floor, and from between foot pads.
- Trim hair from inside ears.
- Tie hair back from face if appropriate (typically for smaller longhaired dogs).
- Clip nails, clean ears, brush teeth.
- Bathe approximately monthly and blow-dry/brush coat smooth.

A Pretty Topknot

The Yorkshire Terrier and Shih Tzu traditionally (in the show ring) have their topknots tied with a ribbon, and the Maltese traditionally gets two ribbons. Other longhaired pets like Lhasa Apsos and Afghans may also enjoy the increased vision, and you may enjoy the crisp appearance of a ribbon-tied topknot.

Shorthaired and Medium Coats

Shorthaired and medium coats are typically denser and thicker than smooth coats, sometimes with undercoats and sometimes without, and are easy to care for; think Labrador Retriever, Norwegian Elkhound, Golden Retriever, German Shepherd Dog, and Welsh Corgi. While shorthaired and medium coats are far easier to brush than longhaired coats, they also tend to shed a lot—some all season long and some approximately twice a year, typically in fall and spring. Nordic dogs like Siberian Huskies, Alaskan Malamutes, and other breeds from colder climates tend to have a much thinner coat during warm weather, so spring and summer can be heavy shedding periods.

Grooming a shorthaired or medium coat is a pleasure. A vigorous brushing with a natural bristle brush or pin brush is all it takes, and shorthaired dogs typically really enjoy a good brush-down. During periods of heavier shedding, a wire slicker brush or other brush designed for a shedding dog can help to remove greater quantities of hair. A good weekly brushing during most of the year and a good daily brushing during shedding periods can drastically reduce the amount of shed hair you will find around the house. Keep ear and foot hair trimmed, teeth clean, and nails short, and you're done!

Shorthaired and medium-coated breeds don't need bathing nearly as often as longhaired breeds because their easy-care coats and the oil glands in their skin keep skin and coat clean. Some are so soil-resistant that they can get very dirty, dry out, and have all the dirt just fall away on its own or with a little help from a bristle brush. The exception is in the case of hunting or water dogs, many of which have short or

Shorthaired Coat Grooming Tools

- all-purpose shampoo or shampoo appropriate to coat color
- blow dryer with low setting
- coat conditioner or lanolin spray
- small scissors
- sturdy natural bristle brush or pin brush
- wire slicker brush

medium coats. These outdoorsy dogs will need bathing more often to keep their coats clean and free of debris, dirt, and bacteria. However, bathing a shorthaired or medium coat too often, especially with a harsh shampoo, can strip the natural oils from coat and skin, making it appear less groomed and less resistant to weather and dirt. Bathe your shorthaired or medium-coated breed every couple of months, unless he gets into something really smelly or too dirty for the coat to self-clean. Use a coat conditioner or lanolin spray made for lubricating skin and coats after a bath to restore suppleness and sheen that may be stripped from the shampoo. Ask your groomer or knowledgeable pet store retailer for product suggestions.

If the weather is chilly, blow-dry your shorthaired or medium-coated dog after bathing. Medium coats in particular can look scruffy if they aren't blown dry. Dense double coats can take a long time to dry. If you don't mind watching your happy pup roll around on the lawn in his newly washed coat, you can let him dry outdoors on a warm sunny day instead of blow-drying, but he may just get dirty all over again. (Of course, he'll have a lot of fun doing it!)

Shorthaired coats are generally easy to care for.

Smooth Coats
Smooth coats are the easiest to groom. Burnished, glossy, hard, slick, and close, smooth coats are both

Smooth Coat Grooming Tools

- all-purpose shampoo or shampoo appropriate to coat color
- coat dressing or lanolin spray
- natural bristle brush or hound glove with natural bristles
- rubber curry comb for large smooth breeds like Boxers, Mastiffs, and Dalmatians
- square of velvet

low-maintenance and gorgeous. Think of a gleaming Boxer, a lustrous Doberman, a polished Pug, or a sleek and shiny Whippet. All smooth breeds, from the aerodynamic Greyhound to the sagaciously droopy Bloodhound, should have a sleek and gleaming coat.

Some smooth coats shed a lot, and some barely at all or only seasonally. In either case, all a smooth coat requires is a weekly brushing with a natural bristle brush or a hound glove to keep the coat smooth and characteristically shiny. Dogs with smooth coats tend to have sensitive skin, so bathing is even less necessary for these breeds than for shorthaired breeds. Twice a year is plenty unless, of

Smooth coats should be sleek and gleaming.

course, your puppy gets into something that just won't brush out. Choose a gentle shampoo for sensitive skin. Shampoos designed to emphasize black or white coats can make the smooth coat even more stunning. End with a rubdown to help redistribute natural skin oils to the coat. You might also add a quick spritz with a lanolin spray or polish the coat with a square of velvet for truly breathtaking and light-catching results.

Trim nails, polish teeth, and that's it. How simple is that?

For Bloodhounds, Basset Hounds, and Coonhounds, it is especially important to clean ears thoroughly with rubbing alcohol and dry well to prevent odor and infection.

Wirehaired Coats

Some people just adore the whiskery, bearded look of the wirehaired dog. Wirehaired Dachshunds, Schnauzers, German Wirehaired Pointers, Wirehaired Pointing Griffons, and many of the terriers, such as the Cairn, Airedale, Border, Welsh, Lakeland, and of course the Wirehaired Fox Terrier, have this unique, coarse wirehaired coat. This weatherproof coat helped farm dogs resist inclement weather conditions and underbrush as they patrolled for vermin.

The wirehaired coat is unique in that it doesn't really shed and instead of regular brushing, it requires a procedure called plucking or stripping to remove the dead hair. Because of its coarse texture, dead hairs don't fall out of the wirehaired coat. After the hairs complete a growth cycle, the dog "blows coat," but unlike fluffier breeds whose soft hair falls out in tufts during a seasonal shed, the wirehaired coat hairs stay put and you or your groomer must pluck them out. If you don't strip a wirehaired

> Many wirehaired coats require plucking (or "stripping") to keep them from becoming tangled or matted.

Wirehaired Coat Grooming Tools

- all-purpose shampoo or shampoo appropriate for wirehaired coats
- clippers for trimming and shaping, or for clipping down the entire coat as an alternative to stripping
- conditioner or baby oil to keep dry hairs from breaking
- pin brush
- scissors for neatening
- stripping knife (optional, if you plan to strip rather than clip your dog)

coat, it can become tangled and matted, compromising both the dog's appearance and health.

Some people choose to clip down their wirehaired pets, and this is an easy way to manage a wirehaired coat if you don't plan to show your dog. Clipping eventually compromises the coarse texture. The coat will become softer and less characteristic, but for a pet dog, this may make no difference at all.

For larger wirehaired dogs like the Scottish Deerhound and the Irish Wolfhound, stripping is unnecessary.

Brush thoroughly with a pin brush to remove excess hair instead. Some people like to strip the long hairs on the ears and belly, but the rest of the coat doesn't require it. The large wirehaired herding breeds like the Giant Schnauzer and the Bouvier des Flandres benefit from an all-over stripping, but again, many pet owners choose to clip these breeds as a much simpler alternative to stripping the substantial coat of a large herding dog.

Whether you decide to clip or strip your wirehaired dog, also brush him regularly with a pin brush, which can remove some of the excess hair, and keep that dry hair coat well conditioned or lubricated by rubbing a small amount of mineral oil between your palms and smoothing it over the coat before brushing to prevent hairs from breaking.

Stripping the Wirehaired Coat

Because stripping is a big job, many who wish to maintain the characteristic hard coat take their wirehaired pets to the groomer. If you want to strip your pet yourself, talk to the breeder or your groomer about the individual method most desirable for your pet, since wirehaired breeds are each groomed according to breed and clipped and scissored into a certain style after bathing and drying. After your dog's outline is in the proper style, you can strip or pluck the coat.

To pluck, work through the entire coat, grasping small tufts of hair and pulling out the dead hairs straight from the roots. Don't twist or pull at an angle or hairs will break off. When done correctly, plucking doesn't hurt your dog, and dogs who are plucked here and there every week (called "rolling" a coat, as an alternative to stripping out all dead hairs seasonally) will be accustomed to and enjoy this grooming. You can also use a stripping knife (ask your groomer to show you how), but plucking is fine and easier to do on a regular basis.

Curly Coats

The curly-coated breeds are among the most difficult to groom. Grooming a curly-coated breed in the correct style is a job for a professional. Unless you plan to keep your frizzy friend clipped down

Curly Coat Grooming Tools

See a professional. Really. A curly-coated breed is super tough to groom. If you really want to learn and are prepared for a time-consuming hobby, have a professional give you a few hands-on lessons and be prepared to make some mistakes, which will, luckily, grow out . . . eventually. Your groomer can also recommend the right tools for your particular pet's curly coat.

(something many pet owners choose for convenience), you *will* want to have your pretty Poodle, corded Puli, powder-puff Bichon, little-lamb Bedlington Terrier, wavy Kerry Blue Terrier, or dreadlocked Komondor professionally groomed.

If you have an Irish Water Spaniel or American Water Spaniel, you may be able to keep the curly coats of these sporting breeds in line on your own with very frequent, thorough brushing to prevent mats, but even these breeds are more easily groomed professionally because groomers are experts at removing mats without damaging coats. Mats are a constant problem in curly-coated breeds, especially for working spaniels.

Ask your groomer how you should maintain your dog between professional grooming and be sure to keep your curly buddy's nails trimmed, teeth cleaned, and ears and eyes immaculate. Even pet clips for Poodles and Bichons are best done professionally. It's worth the extra money, and you can spend the time you save playing with your curly pal.

> Ask your groomer how to maintain your dog's curly coat between visits.

YOUR GROOMING LOG

A grooming log is a handy thing to have. In it, you record, in diary-fashion, what you did and what you found. A grooming log is an essential tool for maintaining your dog's health and can

be a key factor in helping your vet to diagnose a health problem.

Once you've completed your weekly grooming session, whether it is a brief between-professional-grooming maintenance session or a thorough bath-and-comb grooming marathon, record the results in a grooming log.

Remember the grooming exam described at the beginning of the chapter? Keep your grooming log nearby and record anything unusual you find when examining your dog. Did you notice a little bump just behind your Border Collie's right ear? Did your Golden Retriever flinch when you rubbed his tummy? Did your Westie have a red, itchy spot on his left leg? Keep track of anything unusual.

Also make a general note of your dog's coat condition, skin condition, whether you trimmed his nails, cleaned his ears, mopped up his runny eyes, or clipped away any mats. Note whether you found any evidence of a pest problem. Note any special products you used, like pest control, mineral oil on the coat, petroleum jelly to moisten a dry nose, coat whitener, or canine cologne for beautification. Any future allergy conditions could be traced back to products used in grooming, and you might not remember what you used at a future vet visit.

Finally, make some behavioral notes. How much did your dog

Keep a grooming log to record information about grooming sessions, health issues, pet products, and more.

Memory Book

The grooming log is an invaluable tool for keeping track of your dog's health status, but it can also serve as a memory book. In addition to basic care information, also jot any funny stories about your pet. Did he do a neat trick today? Steal your sandwich? Curl up with the cat? Carry your underwear into the dining room mid dinner party? If you record pet stories in your journal, you may someday cherish it as a lovely and touching way to re-experience memories of your pet after he has passed on.

eat and drink today (especially if it varied from the norm)? Did he do anything unusual, such as seem uncharacteristically fatigued, unwilling to go on a walk, unusually sensitive to heat or cold, grumpy or snappy or particularly hyperactive?

Every time you visit your vet, bring along your grooming log. Chances are, you'll be amazed at how handy it is to have all that information recorded for future reference. While you're at it, record every vet visit and everything that was done, from vaccinations and tests to prescribed medication.

Every time you visit your vet, bring along your grooming log.

5

TRAINING AND SOCIALIZATION FOR A HEALTHY LIFE

Although this isn't a training book, you may wonder what dog training has to do with health. Nothing you do for your dog will have a greater impact on his health and welfare than being well trained and well socialized. Behavioral problems are a major reason why pet dogs are relinquished to animal shelters, and a dog in a shelter is probably not headed down the road of good health and a long life. Sadly, many puppies never see their first birthday because they weren't trained and got into more trouble than their owners were willing to handle. If you don't teach your puppy what kind of behavior is acceptable to humans, he won't be successful living with humans. It's as simple as that.

We humans aren't very tolerant of bad or even normal canine behavior. Our untrained canine friends may bark to alert us of every suspicious piece of trash that blows down the street. They may use the house as a bathroom because that's what we do, right? They may chew on our shoes when we aren't home because it reminds them of us. And what do we do? We get angry, they get confused, the behavior worsens, and many of us, sad to say, give up. A badly behaved puppy won't grow up to be a well-behaved and successful

> **Training gives dogs and humans a mutual "language" through which to communicate.**

human companion . . . and may not grow up at all.

That's why it is absolutely essential to train your dog, preferably in a professional setting.

HOW TO TRAIN A DOG

Dog training may sound easy, but many who come home with a dog for the first time don't have the first idea how to start. If you've seen those dogs on television trotting neatly around the show ring, leaping over hurdles in an agility race, or sitting, lying down, and shaking hands on command, you may wonder how on earth anyone was ever able to communicate the information about what they wanted to a creature who doesn't speak your language.

In essence, communication is exactly what dog training is all about. Because dogs don't speak and we aren't practiced in the nuances of canine communication, training gives dogs and humans a mutual sort of "language" through which to communicate.

There are many different methods of training. Clicker training, lure and reward training, and traditional or "military" training are a few of the most popular. If you aren't a professional trainer, however, you may find it difficult to grasp the concepts behind these different methods, which are concepts rooted in the study of canine behavior. That's why it's best to begin

Training Techniques

Clicker training is a type of training that uses a little handheld plastic box with a metal tab that makes a clicking sound when pressed. The trainer uses the click to precisely mark a behavior, and the behavior is then rewarded. Clicker training separates the reward from the behavior with the precise sound of the click, making it perfectly clear to your dog which behaviors you like. *Lure-and-reward* training uses a treat to lure a dog into certain behaviors like *sit*, *down*, *come*, and even through obstacle course equipment. *Traditional* or *military training* is the older style of dog training in which dogs are taught commands through repetition and are corrected for mistakes, usually with a so-called "choke" chain. This type of training uses intimidation and force to teach a dog what to do. It can work, but most trainers today have discarded these old methods in favor of *positive-reinforcement training*, which focuses on rewarding good behavior and setting dogs up to succeed. Positive-reinforcement training fosters a more positive bond between you and your dog. Look for a trainer who uses positive-reinforcement techniques.

at the beginning—that's where your puppy is beginning, too.

Puppy Kindergarten

Puppy kindergarten classes are a great way to begin socializing and training your new puppy. These informal classes don't focus on hardcore training. Instead, they act more as an aid to socialization. A group of people bring in their puppies, and everyone gets to interact, learn about basic dog care and training, and expose the puppies to lots of different people, and of course, other dogs.

Puppy kindergarten classes are available in most cities and towns.

They are positive and fun in character and everyone has a great time, sometimes forging lifelong friendships with others whose dogs get along. Consider it a structured and educational playgroup for puppies.

Puppy kindergarten classes are a great way to begin socializing and training your puppy.

Basic Obedience

Once your puppy has graduated from puppy kindergarten, it's time to move on to basic obedience. If you never take another class, don't skip this one. This is the class where you and your dog will learn how to communicate what you would like him to do. Because most dogs are highly motivated to please their owners, not to mention doing whatever it takes to get a tasty treat, some simple techniques make it easy for you to show your dog what you mean by "sit," "stay," "come," and other essentials.

In basic obedience, you and your dog construct the bare bones of training communication that will allow you to either move on to more advanced training, if you enjoy it, or simply communicate more successfully at home. Basic obedience instructors typically teach you how to train your dog to sit, lie down, stay, come, and walk next to you without pulling on the leash. You will also get helpful hints about advanced training and typical behavior problems. You'll learn a lot, and if you find a good instructor, basic obedience classes are worth every penny.

A good obedience instructor is someone who uses positive methods but is flexible enough

Basic obedience instructors teach you how to train your dog for basic commands.

to adapt or switch methods if one method isn't working for you and your dog. If your trainer is adamant that all dogs respond best to clicker training, for example, you may find that you and your dog won't be successful in class.

Watch a couple of classes if possible before you sign up, and get recommendations, too. When watching classes or talking to friends who have taken classes, look for a few key signs that you've found a good obedience instructor:

• Do the people and the dogs seem to be having a good time? If the class isn't fun, neither you nor your dog will keep up with the necessary practice.

• Does the instructor use positive reinforcement methods and rewards to teach dogs, or does she use harsh words, choke chains, and force? Instructors using positive reinforcement techniques are usually better for pet dogs and their people.

• Is the instructor friendly, with good people skills? Even if she loves dogs more than anything else

> Dogs should master basic obedience before moving on to advanced competitions.

in the world and is able to train dogs herself to the highest levels of competitive obedience, an instructor who can't communicate well with people or who doesn't enjoy people probably won't do a good job at training you. People training is just as important in basic obedience as dog training (or arguably even more important).

- Does the instructor obviously enjoy her job? An irritable or impatient instructor is unpleasant to work with.
- Do you like the way the instructor interacts with the dogs? If you feel like the instructor is too rough on the dogs, or if you aren't comfortable with the methods you see, look elsewhere. You probably haven't found the class for you.

Basic obedience is essential for every dog because it gives humans and their dogs a set of rules and signs through which they can come to an understanding. This is how everybody learns how to live together. If you decide to continue on to more advanced canine competitions, like competitive obedience, agility (a competition where dogs run an obstacle course), flyball (a fast-paced canine relay race), or even the show ring, you and your dog must first master the basics. After all, you can't play a piano concerto unless you first learn your scales!

But even if you aren't interested in moving on to competition with your friend, basic obedience is the key to a society in which dogs are well-behaved and well managed by their owners. This is the key to decreasing the number of dog attacks and dog nuisance problems that give so many dogs and dog owners a bad name. More dogs would be allowed in parks, on beaches, in hotels, and in apartments if they were better behaved, and basic obedience is the first step toward demonstrating to the world that your dog is a good citizen.

While learning basic training under the personal guidance of an experienced obedience instructor is usually best, you can set the groundwork for basic obedience moves on your own using these tips. Some of these methods may not work for every dog, but young puppies will usually respond well.

Sit

Take a piece of kibble or a tiny bit of hot dog or cheese and hold it in front of your puppy's nose so that he gets a good whiff. Then slowly move the treat up and over his head. He'll have to sit to see it. When he does, say, "Sit," then praise him and give him the treat. Repeat and he'll soon associate the movement with the word. For a long *sit*, keep him sitting for slightly longer periods of time before giving him the treat. Always let him succeed—give him the treat just before he is ready to give up and stand up again.

Down

Lure your puppy into a *sit*, then pull the treat out and move it down as you say the word "down." As he follows the treat with his nose, he'll have to creep forward. Help guide him into a lying-down position with your other hand while keeping the treat about an inch (2.5 cm) in front of his nose. For a long *down*, say, "Down," as he goes down and then maintain eye contact, increasing the time by about 30 seconds each time you practice, before giving him the treat. Always let him succeed by giving him the treat before he gives up and stands again. Sometimes you have to sense when this is about to happen.

Stay

After your puppy has mastered *sit* and *down*, lure him into one of these positions, then hold your palm up and say, "Stay." Take one step away. If he jumps up, put him back into position and again say, "Stay," with your palm up. Only make him stay a couple of seconds the first time. Then step forward, praise him, and give him the treat. Extend the *stay* time for a couple of seconds and step back another step every few times. Go back to your puppy to give him the treat rather than having him come to you at first so that he doesn't confuse the *stay* with *come*. With this method, your buddy will be specifically rewarded for staying and not for coming to you.

Canine Competition

Basic obedience classes frequently offer introductions to competitive obedience, agility, conformation shows, and other fun canine competitions. The obedience instructor may explain how these competitions work or even let you and your dog try out agility equipment. Basic obedience is necessary for any advanced canine competition, so get the basics down first, then consider the possibilities for future fun together by enlisting in a local obedience or agility club and buddying up to those experienced in the canine sport of your choice.

Come

Teach your puppy the *come* command by practicing many times each day. Call him to you, using your verbal cue "come," and reward him with a toy, a treat, or lots of affection when he comes. Eventually you can combine *stay* and *come* by making your puppy stay, stepping back, and then releasing him with a word of your choice. Then let him come to get the treat.

Walk Nicely on Leash

Laboring to drag (or be dragged) by a dog down the street is no fun, but how do you get a dog to walk nicely next to you when all he wants to do is run, or sniff, or tie you up in the leash while he wanders in circles around and behind you? Two or three times every day, take your dog out on a walk with a pocketful of small treats. Start out with your dog on your right side, leash held loosely. Say, "Walk," and move forward. The second your dog starts to pull or lags behind, stop. Look straight ahead and ignore him completely. Soon he will look to see why you aren't moving. Get him into position, say, "Good dog!" and start walking again. Every time he gets out of position, stop walking and completely ignore him. Dogs hate being ignored and will wrack their brains to figure out what you want. It may take a few weeks, but eventually most dogs will learn that when they stay next to you, they get to move, and when they get out of line, they have to stop. Be consistent and diligent about this and you will soon have a dog who behaves on a leash—the envy of the neighborhood!

Canine Good Citizen® Program

When competitive obedience first became an event, the purpose was for dogs and their people to demonstrate what good manners they had. In fact, the basic obedience title is called a CD, which stands for "companion dog," meaning that a dog who has earned this title has all the qualities of a good companion.

As obedience progressed and became more competitive, another program emerged that allows "regular" (in other words, not necessarily purebred) pets, no matter their breed or age, to demonstrate that they, too, can be good canine citizens. The American Kennel Club's Canine Good Citizen (CGC) program awards a nice certificate and the CGC title to dogs who pass a 10-item test administered all over the country by trained evaluators. You and your dog can master the 10 basic tests in a basic obedience class or in widely available Canine Good Citizen training classes.

Who's Training Whom?

A dog trainer is the person training a dog, so if you and your dog take an obedience class together, you will be the dog trainer. The person teaching you *and* your dog how to communicate is the obedience instructor. If you hire someone to train your dog for you, that person is also called a trainer. This can be handy, and particularly effective for problem dogs, but in most cases, your relationship with your dog will benefit most if you are the trainer, not someone else who won't live with your dog. After all, isn't that why you got a dog, for the relationship? Work through the training together and you'll both be closer, more knowledgeable, and better behaved when interacting with each other.

Want to get a head start on a CGC for your dog? The following are the 10 tests. If your dog fails any one of these tests, he will be dismissed but can try the test again on a different day as many different times as necessary.

Test Item 1: Accepting a friendly stranger.

Your dog must stay in position next to you and behave, i.e., not act shy or resentful, when the evaluator approaches and shakes your hand in a friendly manner.

Test Item 2: Sitting politely for petting.

Your dog must stand in place and allow the evaluator to pet him in a friendly way without acting shy or resentful.

Test Item 3: Appearance and grooming.

Your dog must be in good health and stand politely for brushing, combing, and a physical examination of his ears and feet by the evaluator.

Test Item 4: Out for a walk on a loose lead.

Your dog must walk beside you on either side on a leash and remain attentive and responsive to you as you

The Canine Good Citizen (CGC) program involves 10 basic obedience tests, such as the *down*.

walk him around the testing area, following the evaluator's directions for a right turn, a left turn, an about turn, and a stop and start, with or without sitting during the stops.

Test Item 5: Walking through a crowd.

Your dog must walk on a leash next to you through an area containing pedestrian traffic without getting overly excited, shy, or resentful, and without jumping on anyone or straining on the leash.

Test Item 6: *Sit* and *down* on command and staying in place.

Your dog must show that he can sit and lie down on command. Then, with your dog on a 20-foot (6-m) leash, you must tell him to stay and walk forward to the length of the leash, turn, and return back to your dog. Your dog must stay in place when you do this until you release him at the evaluator's cue.

Test Item 7: Coming when called.

Your dog must stay while you walk away for 10 feet (3 m) and then turn to face him. When you call your dog, he must come to you.

> Dogs must sit politely for petting, accept friendly strangers, and perform other tasks to earn the Canine Good Citizen (CGC) title.

Test Item 8: Reaction to another dog.

Your dog must be polite and show no more than casual interest in another dog as another handler and dog come up to you in a friendly manner and stop, shake hands, and chat. Neither dog should move to go to the other dog or to the handlers during this test.

Test Item 9: Reaction to distraction.

Your dog must remain confident and interested or curious or even slightly startled by distractions, such as a jogger, another canine, or a rolling dolly. Your dog must not react in a panicked, aggressive, or overly startled manner and should not bark at the distraction.

Test Item 10: Supervised separation.

Your dog must tolerate supervision by a trusted person. The evaluator will approach you in a friendly manner and ask you if you would like her to watch your dog. You agree, and then the evaluator takes the leash. You must then go out of sight of your dog for three minutes. Your dog needn't maintain a position but should not bark, whine, or pace unnecessarily or act otherwise nervous or traumatized. Mild agitation and nervousness are permitted.

That's the test. Easy? Sure it is, with the right obedience training and lots of practice. All tests are performed on

It's your job as a canine guardian to make house rules clear.

a leash and may be inside or outside. And remember, you can always try the test again . . . and again . . . and again, until your buddy has earned the prestigious title of CGC.

HOUSE RULES

One of the most important things pet owners learn during puppy kindergarten and basic obedience is how to teach a dog some basic house rules. No puppy (or human for that matter) is born knowing what is and isn't appropriate in the house, so it's your job as a canine guardian to make those rules clear.

As mentioned at the beginning of this chapter, behavioral problems are one of the main reasons that dogs end up in animal shelters, but in most cases, if your dog doesn't know the house rules, the owner is at fault. Once again, classes are incredibly important because the obedience instructor trains both you and your dog about how to interact and communicate. If you have proven-effective strategies to help housetrain, control excessive barking and chewing, and fix other non-human-friendly doggy behaviors, you'll be set up to succeed.

While classes are usually the best environment for any dog–human team to learn together, here are some helpful hints and strategies for controlling some common canine behaviors you probably don't like very much. Just remember, every dog–human team is different. What works for one dog may not work for another, so be flexible, patient, and positive in your approach. Eventually you'll find a method that works for both of you.

Oops, He Did It Again!

The one thing puppies do that most irritates humans has to be those unfortunate accidents of elimination . . . you know, those little "surprises" your puppy leaves for you when you aren't paying attention, and those little

Housetraining requires patience and consistency.

Teacher's Pet

Many good books and videos give you directions for training your dog, but in my opinion, there is no substitute for a hands-on class or private sessions with a great dog trainer who can watch you and your dog and give you personalized suggestions and corrections. Look for a trainer who uses positive rather than punitive measures and who is flexible enough to adapt training styles to meet the needs of you and your dog. Let books, dog magazines, and videos serve as supplementary information because, of course, the more you know, the better a dog trainer you'll be.

puddles all over the kitchen floor in the morning.

Puppies have no idea where it is appropriate to eliminate, but think about it: neither do human babies. We put diapers on them for a couple of years, and many parents struggle to "potty train" their kids. Your puppy presents a similar challenge, but fortunately for you, puppies usually learn housetraining a lot faster than toddlers learn to use a toilet. Your smart little pup will figure out where it's okay to go and where it's not okay to go in a matter of just a few months. Some quick studies learn within a few weeks of bringing them

Crate training is one of the most reliable housetraining methods.

home. (This also depends on the age of your puppy when you bring him home, how much housetraining the breeder or previous owners have already accomplished, and what breed you have.)

Patience is certainly in order when it comes to housetraining your puppy, but don't expect your pup to figure out the rules all by himself. Some handy tools and helpful rules will get your puppy in shape in no time, and the most powerful housetraining tool you can have is a crate.

A crate is great! Choose a plastic or wire crate just big enough for puppy to sit, stand, turn around, and lie down in, but not so big that he can soil in one side and sleep in another. Some companies make pet carriers that conveniently fold up for easy storage.

Crate training is one of the most reliable housetraining methods, and it's simple. Dogs love to have a den-like area where they can go for downtime whenever they need it. Because dogs don't soil where they sleep, keep your puppy in his crate whenever you cannot directly supervise him.

Of course, that doesn't mean leaving him in there all day long. No puppy can hold it for more than a few hours, and you'll just be setting him up to fail. Puppies should come into a home where someone is often around and can watch and direct most of the time, but when it's nap time or you need to get something

Tiny Tyrants

Toy dogs are notoriously more difficult to housetrain than larger dogs, possibly because their owners tend to indulge them and also because tiny puddles and itty-bitty poops aren't as easy to notice. Most toy breeds will learn eventually, however, as long as you do the work to catch them in the act and take them outside on a schedule. Toy dogs need to go out more often than large dogs (tiny dogs have tiny bladders), but a trip to the yard every hour or two in the beginning will pay off quickly later on. Besides, toy dogs need outdoor time, regular walks, and yard play, too. The more they are outside, the more quickly they will realize that's where the bathroom is. (Don't forget to praise every time they do it right!)

done, put him in his comfy crate and shut the door. He may cry at first, but he'll soon learn to see his crate as a place of refuge *as long as you never use the crate for punishment*. Let it be a haven.

When your puppy is out of his crate, watch him carefully for sniffing and circling behavior, then take him quickly outside to the spot you'd like to train him to use for his personal potty. When he goes, associate the action with a word. (Pick one you won't regret later— "potty" is okay, but some other words I can think of could prove awkward

should the neighbors overhear.)

When he does his duty, praise him effusively. Always take your puppy out about a half hour after eating (sooner if he starts to circle and sniff), and as soon as you take him out of his crate. Wait outside with him until he goes so that you can mark the behavior with the word and then deliver the praise. A few weeks of this and he should get the idea. If you are consistent and always watching, he'll learn quickly.

If you fail your pup by missing his signals, and he has an accident in the house, *it's your fault*. Please don't blame your puppy. He won't understand why you are angry, and you could seriously damage your relationship. Remember to communicate with him through methods he understands. If he knows where you want him to eliminate, that's what he'll do, unless he absolutely can't hold it any longer, you don't get the signal to let him out, or he simply doesn't yet understand what you want.

Scolding a dog for having an accident doesn't work and hurts your relationship.

Play Biting and Chewing

Everyone with a puppy knows about those needle-sharp teeth. Puppy bites hurt! The problem is that your puppy doesn't know that. Puppies play together, biting and chewing on their littermates, and because dog skin is less sensitive than human skin, the other pups don't seem to mind much. We humans, on the other hand, don't like puppy bites, but pet owners often tend to overlook the irritation of those sharp little teeth because the puppy is just so darned cute.

Bad idea.

Dogs must learn at an early age that biting human skin is a big NO. That means reacting with a sharp sound and pulling back every single time the puppy's teeth hit human skin. Your puppy won't like this startling reaction, and it teaches your puppy bite inhibition. An adult dog with bite inhibition who is well socialized to lots of different kinds of people will be far less likely to bite.

As for chewing, some breeds and some individual dogs are more apt to chew destructively than others, but in general, you can prevent your dog from chewing destructively by doing a few simple things:

- Give your dog plenty of toys he is allowed to chew. Make sure some are challenging, like stuffable toys filled with treats or peanut butter or other temptations that are mentally as well as orally stimulating.
- Keep your dog busy! Bored dogs are more likely to engage in destructive chewing. Up your dog's daily exercise and give him more attention.
- When you can't supervise your dog, let him rest in his crate or in a safe place where he can't destroy anything.
- Don't leave your dog alone for more than a few hours, though. Come home from work on your

When some breeds grow into adult dogs, their jumping-up behaviors can start knocking people over.

Puppy Party

Socializing your dog is one of the best ways to keep him well-adjusted. After your pup has had his first few rounds of vaccinations, host a puppy party. Invite lots of different people of various ages and appearances to come to your house and meet your dog. Let people pet him and talk to him one at a time while you supervise so that every human interaction is positive. But don't stop there. Take your puppy with you whenever you go out (when possible) so that he is also exposed to different places and different situations. The more positive and varied experiences he has in the first year, the more well-adjusted, flexible, and stable he will be.

lunch hour to take him on a walk or hire a dog walker to do it for you. Remember, wear him out, and he'll be too tired to chew your shoes.

Keep shoes and other things you don't want your dog to chew out of his reach.

- Keep your shoes and other things you don't want your dog to chew out of his reach. Prevention of the behavior always works best.

Jumping Up

Dogs love to be with us, and when we get home after a long day, they want to see us . . . up close! Puppies often learn that jumping up on their owners is just fine. We are flattered that our cute, fuzzy little fellows love us so much that they practically try to climb up to get to us.

However, when that fuzzy little fellow grows to be a 75-pound (34-kg) bruiser, jumping up isn't so cute. It can even be dangerous, especially to a small child or an elderly or petite adult. Just as puppies must learn bite inhibition early, they must also learn that jumping won't get them anything good, but that sitting politely will.

The problem with this lesson is that it's hard for humans to teach. When we get home after a busy day, a dog jumping on us is likely to get our attention, even if that attention is negative and involves lots of yelling. That's still attention to your dog and preferable to being ignored. A nice polite dog who sits patiently is easy to ignore or forget about, so we inadvertently tend to reinforce the jumping up with attention, while failing to reinforce the behavior we so prize.

Starting in puppyhood, when your puppy jumps on you it is crucial to either completely ignore him or tell him, "No," firmly and tell him to sit. When he sits, lavish him with praise and give him the attention he craves. If jumping up is never rewarded in any way, including with yelling, your

Dogs have been bred over the centuries to bark for different reasons.

dog will soon stop doing it. If sitting nicely for petting when greeting people is always rewarded, that's exactly what your dog will learn to do. Dogs are smart. They know what they want. Make it easy for them to understand how they can get your attention, and they'll behave just the way you would like them to.

Barking . . . and Barking . . . and Barking

Most dogs bark. All dogs make some kind of noise, even the so-called "barkless" Basenji. Dogs have been bred over the centuries to bark for different reasons. Herding dogs bark to keep the flocks in line. Terriers bark to indicate where that pesky vermin is hiding. Hounds bark to indicate that they have found what they were looking for. Guardian dogs (most dogs, for that matter) bark to warn of intruders.

Barking is integral to what a dog is, and that means that to some extent, if you plan to live with a dog, you have to put up with some barking. On the other hand, there is a limit.

Just like people, some dogs are pretty intuitive about when barking is really necessary and when it's not. They may bark if a stranger approaches the property but will completely ignore the blue jay in the tree because they know it isn't a threat and they aren't going to be able to get to it, anyway. Other dogs tend to be a bit more . . . shall we say chatty? They bark at everything— any people, anywhere; any other dogs; local wildlife; dog toys; wind; air. Some breeds are more prone to excessive barking. Terriers tend to be particularly "barky," making them less well suited for apartment living, especially when the walls are thin and the neighbors aren't amused by the sound of constant barking—can you say "eviction notice?"

Then there are dogs who get in the habit of barking, and it becomes almost like a compulsive behavior. Other dogs are simply bored. They don't have anything else to do and they enjoy barking, so they do it. Still other dogs are nervous, either because they are unsocialized or are left alone too often, and become fanatical about the approach of anything to their property, barking frantically at any movement. These

Bark Stress

Excessive barking can actually damage your dog's health by injuring his vocal chords. Perhaps even more insidiously, excessive barking, especially when it becomes obsessive and chronic, creates extreme stress in a dog and could contribute to an anxiety disorder. (Yep, dogs can get those!) Of course, if your dog is barking out of boredom or separation anxiety or due to a health problem, first resolve the problem, which could be causing your dog much more stress than the actual barking symptom.

last few types of barkers have problems you can address.

Because you can indeed be evicted or otherwise charged when your dog becomes a legitimate nuisance to your neighbors, and because compulsive or excessive barking is actually stressful on your dog and can result in ill health, you must, as a responsible dog owner, help your dog stop excessive barking. You can do this in several ways:

- Stop rewarding your dog for barking. You might not realize you are doing this, but if your dog barks and you yell at him to cut it out, he may interpret your yelling as reinforcement, almost as if you are barking in agreement. Instead, quietly and calmly remove him from the source and put him in his kennel or in a room alone. When he is quiet, praise him.

Scolding your barking dog reinforces the barking behavior.

- Keep your dog busy. This is one of the best ways to minimize barking. Give him more interesting things to do. Spend more time together when you are home, and when you are away, provide things to play with, like toys stuffed with treats, and other things to do—maybe even a visit from a dog walker.
- Doggy daycare is another great option, and it's increasingly

popular, available, and affordable. It's perfect for dogs who would otherwise spend the day alone.

- If you won't be away for more than two or three hours, keep your dog in his crate so he can't get to the window. His "den" will keep him calmer, and he won't feel responsible for having to scare away all those "intruders" he sees passing on the street. He'll probably just sleep.
- Make sure your dog gets lots of exercise before you leave for the day. This is also highly effective because a tired dog is a good dog. A long morning walk can help a lot.

- Minimize bark-inducing stimuli. Don't let your dog sit and look out the window if it makes him bark too much. If you see another dog approaching on a walk or someone walking by your yard and your dog starts to get excited, immediately call him to come to you and have him sit. Pet him calmly and praise him. Hold his collar and reassure him that you saw the approaching intruder and he has done his job. If he struggles and barks, don't

> Good exercise can mellow out a consistently barking dog.

get excited and "bark back" again. Remain uninteresting and non-interactive until he is quiet again.

- Don't leave your dog outside and ignore him for long periods of time if he tends to stand outside and bark or patrol the property line obsessively. Let him be inside with you. He'd rather be there, anyway.

Digging and Other Destruction

Some dogs love to dig, particularly terriers (terrier means "earth dog"), but hounds, working breeds, and herding breeds are notorious diggers, too. Any breed and any dog may enjoy digging. It's fun, it's interesting, it's satisfying. What's not to love?

At least that's your dog's point of view. If you have flowerbeds or even just a nice lawn, you aren't going to want your dog to dig it up. Holes from digging are hazardous to human ankles and don't exactly contribute to a lovely landscape.

Some dogs are dedicated diggers, but you can usually at least reduce, if not eliminate, digging behavior with a few key strategies:

- Keep your dog well exercised and busy. Many dogs dig because they have excess energy or because they are bored.
- Give your dogs challenging things to do. If they are mentally stimulated with toys from which they must work to extract treats

> Digging behaviors can be reduced or eliminated with a few key strategies.

or from complex training sessions with you, they will be less likely to feel the need to dig.

- Keep your dog inside when you aren't supervising him in the yard.
- Fence off areas tempting to your dog, such as flowerbeds and vegetable gardens.
- If you are building a fence, pour concrete along the base to keep your dog from digging under, or at least bury the fence 6–12 inches (15.5–30.5 cm) underground (depending on how persistent a digger your dog is).

Fear and Anxiety

If your dog is fearful, either around new situations, people, and noises or if he's always afraid of the same thing (fireworks, the vacuum cleaner, you leaving him), that fear is harmful to his health because it causes him so much stress. It is also damaging to your relationship. Fear makes dogs do things we don't like, such as suffer housetraining accidents, destroy things, claw madly at doors, whine and cry, or cling to us, pathetically shivering. Some dogs can also become fear biters who will attack out of panic. That means someone could get seriously injured, you could get in big legal trouble,

Fear and anxiety can foster aggression and destructive behavior.

and your dog, sad to say, might pay the ultimate price.

Many different methods exist for conquering fear and anxiety in dogs. Some behaviorists recommend desensitization, in which the animal is exposed to noises, strangers, or whatever the source of fear is just a little at a time. This method works on the same principle as socialization for puppies but is probably best practiced under the supervision of a professional canine behaviorist, behavioral consultant, or experienced trainer. The more your dog is exposed to something, the more familiar and the less scary it becomes, but you don't want to make the problem worse.

In extreme cases of fear or anxiety, your vet may also want to prescribe medication to help calm your dog.

The more your dog is exposed to something, the more familiar it becomes.

However, in the case of separation anxiety, a condition in which your dog becomes fearful and often destructive when you leave, it is best handled a bit differently. Experts suggest ignoring your dog for the 10 minutes before you leave and the 10 minutes after you come home. Although you may find this difficult to do, this process sends your dog the message that your coming and going aren't exciting or stressful or overly emotional in any way. Big shows of affection, petting, and fawning over your dog ("Is Zuzu going to MISS Mommy when she goes away? Because Zuzu LOVES Mommy? Yes she does! Yes she does!") will only make these transitions more emotional and stressful for your dog.

When you do come home, after you have ignored your dog for about 10 minutes, then you can give him a pat on the head, a few kind words. Work up to the smushy kissy affection after you've been home for a while, so that your buddy doesn't associate it with your leaving or coming home.

Again, for severe separation anxiety, see your vet. Your dog could have an underlying medical problem or might require medication to help relax him so that you can better treat the problem.

On the Run

Do you call your dog Harry Houdini because he can escape from everywhere? Whether they leap over fences in a single bound or can dig out like the

Responsible pet owners keep their dogs from running away.

Poky Little Puppy, some dogs have an unquenchable wanderlust. Of course, a loose dog is in great danger. Your wayward pup could be hit by a car, stolen, or attacked by another dog or even a wild animal. The best way to keep your pet from escaping is simply to thwart him. As a responsible pet owner, you must keep your pet from running free, even if it means extending the height of your fence, pouring concrete around the base of your fence, or taking your dog on long walks instead of letting him roam around the backyard unsupervised.

And if you don't have a fence? Please keep your dog safe and don't let him out without a leash.

> A well-trained dog has a great start to a long, happy life.

When You Just Gotta Dig

Sometimes it's easier to go with the flow and give your dog a chance to dig. Designate an area, perhaps a plastic swimming pool filled with sand or a square of dirt marked off by railroad ties, for your dog to dig. If he learns that digging in his special area is okay, he'll be able to exercise his need to dig without upsetting you. Everybody wins!

A GREAT START

Trained, socialized, well-behaved? Your dog has a great start to a long, healthy life. Keep up that training and keep building that relationship and you'll both enjoy your time together even more.

PART THREE

PLAN FOR A

HEALTHY LIFE

6

PUPPY HEALTH AND WELLNESS

Puppies: They are so adorable, and yet . . . so much work! Life with a new puppy isn't all cute doggy kisses and cuddles and hilarious videos you can't wait to post on your favorite social media account. It also involves choosing the right dog for you, getting the right early vet care, and making some important decisions about the house rules and how you and your dog will create a positive relationship.

A good beginning for a happy, healthy puppy comes from good breeding, proper health care, thorough socialization, bonding with you, and lots of fun and friendly training. The best place to start, of course, is with a healthy puppy. This chapter will help you to find a healthy puppy with great potential and help you to put into place those health and behavior habits that will last you and your dog a lifetime.

> Healthy puppies come from good breeding, proper health care, thorough socialization, bonding with you, and fun and friendly training.

CHOOSING A HEALTHY PUPPY
Where do you find a healthy puppy? Considering that every year in the US, more dogs are born than humans, healthy puppies are everywhere. Unfortunately, so are unhealthy, badly bred, unsocialized puppies.

Finding a healthy puppy isn't just a matter of getting lucky. How do you know you are choosing a puppy with great health? The best way is to know exactly where your puppy came from, and there are several ways to get this crucial information. One is by buying your puppy from a quality breeder who can not only tell you but show you exactly where your puppy came from by letting you meet the puppy's parents and even other relatives like uncles, aunts, and grandparents. They will also be able to provide records of health tests and vaccinations, and hold frank discussions about what they do to socialize their puppies.

Another option is to find a puppy at a shelter or from a rescue group that carefully monitors and tests the dogs who are relinquished. Some families have to give up their pets due to reasons they can't help and provide full information on the dog's past. Many dogs in shelters and with rescue groups are given thorough veterinary examinations and behavior tests, and are neutered if necessary. Shelter and rescue workers are also often very experienced and good at analyzing a dog's temperament and tendencies. However, in some areas and cities, shelters and rescue groups are overwhelmed and understaffed. In these cases, dogs with problem behaviors might slip through the cracks and you might not know until you bring your dog home that you are dealing with a serious issue. This is not to discourage a shelter adoption—most of these dogs make excellent pets, with a little work. They are fixer-uppers, in the best sense.

You can do certain tests and make certain observations on your own,

Your Social Butterfly

Socialization, as used in this book, is the process of introducing positive associations to your puppy via many different stimuli so that he learns from the beginning that people, places, and distractions are generally good, rather than something to be feared or attacked. Young puppies should meet many different people of all ages, genders, sizes, colors, and shapes, as well as other dogs and other pets. They should be exposed to many different situations, from parking lots and the outsides of stores with automatic doors to dog parks, soccer games, and the neighborhood. Socialization teaches puppies to be good citizens with even temperaments, but it will not erase protective instincts in dogs who are naturally protective. Socializing your dog will not take away his ability to be a good guard dog. Instead, it will teach him the subtleties of life so that he will be more equipped to tell good from bad, friend from intruder.

too, although whenever getting a dog from a shelter or rescue group, you can never know firsthand what has happened in that dog's past. Many people say their shelter dogs are the most well-behaved, even seemingly grateful dogs they ever had. Once in a while, however, a dog from a shelter can be unpredictable.

Of course, simply buying from a breeder doesn't guarantee that you'll get a healthy dog. First, find a quality breeder whose ideals match yours, who is knowledgeable and communicative, and whom you feel you can trust. Do your own research, too, so you aren't completely at the breeder's mercy for information. Knowing what makes a breeder

good and what red flags may signal a less-than-quality breeder can help you to find the breeder that is right for you.

Helping disadvantaged pets is noble, but living with a sick or temperamental dog can be incredibly stressful.

Finding a Breeder

Lots of people breed dogs, and most people who have never bought a dog from a breeder before (and some who have) don't have any idea what makes a good breeder. The first dog I ever bought was from a backyard breeder who was not socializing or taking very good care of her dogs, but I didn't know any better. I thought all breeders' facilities looked like that—crowded rows of small wire kennels filled with oversized Miniature Pinschers yapping hysterically, puppies missing patches of hair, and a general air of chaos and filth— because I had never seen anything different. If only I had known then what I know now, after years of meeting and interviewing breeders and seeing the good, the bad, and the downright ugly, I would have run in the opposite direction! (That Miniature Pinscher was timid, a fear biter, and had epilepsy, by the way.)

Because of the Internet, potential pet owners now have access to hundreds of breeders, so even if you are set on a Papillon or a Beauceron or a Catahoula Leopard Dog and nobody is breeding them in your area, you can probably get one.

But having access to breeders all over the country, even the world, makes screening breeders for quality and responsibility even more difficult. Even so, I've discovered that there are certain qualities really good breeders generally have in common and certain red flags that often indicate

a substandard breeder. Some of these you can find out about through email or phone communication, but in most cases, you should take a trip and visit the breeder in person. Really particular breeders will usually make you do this anyway.

In general, however, looking out for the qualities on the "Good Breeder" list and steering clear of the qualities on the "Not-So-Good Breeder" list can help you make a more informed decision about the breeder who is right for you.

The Good Breeder List

You're on your way to visit the breeder of the puppy you hope you will bring home with you. But how do you know that breeder is doing a good job?

> When getting a dog from a shelter, you often won't know what happened in his past.

Check for the following qualities, answers, and conditions in your breeder and her facility. If the breeder you visit measures up to these criteria, you've probably got a gem. Start getting to know those puppies!

- First impressions first. The breeder is friendly, open, and gives the impression of honesty. Sure, some people can seem friendly and honest even if they aren't, but listen to your gut. Do you trust this person?
- The breeder seems to know a lot about the breed. Ask questions about the breed's temperament, health issues, energy level, and history, even if you already know.

The breeder should know at least as much as you do about the breed, and ideally will know much more from her years of experience.

In most cases, you should take a trip and visit a dog breeder in person.

- In addition to the good qualities of the breed, the breeder also tells you all the challenges and downsides to the breed in order to fully prepare you for the commitment ahead.
- The breeder breeds only one or possibly two similar breeds.
- The breeder has been in the business for many years or, if just starting, is working closely with experienced breeders with good reputations.

- The breeder shows you evidence of health tests performed on the parents of the litter, such as hips and elbows certified free of dysplasia through the Orthopedic Foundation for Animals (OFA) and eyes certified free of progressive retinal atrophy through the Canine Eye Registration Foundation (CERF). If your breed has the gene for piebald coloration (large patches of two or more colors, usually including white), such as a Dalmatian, Bull Terrier, Beagle, or English Setter, ask the breeder whether she has had the puppies brainstem-auditory-evoked-response (BAER) tested for deafness.
- The breeder is happy to give you the number of her vet and other references. (Check them!)
- The breeder grills you about where you live, whether you have children, whether you have a fence, why you want this particular breed, whether you've raised a puppy before, and other questions you might consider none of her business. That means the breeder cares about where her puppies will go and doesn't want to put them in a bad situation. That's a great quality in a breeder, so don't be offended.
- The breeder raises the puppies in the house where they can be in frequent contact with humans.

Breeder Knows Best

What if you spend a lot of time with a breeder and then she refuses to sell you a puppy? This happens frequently with responsible breeders who won't sell puppies to homes that they don't believe are suited for their precious charges. Maybe you have boisterous children too young to safely handle a delicate Pomeranian puppy. Maybe you don't have a fence and the breeder knows that a Siberian Husky will be long gone within a matter of weeks. Maybe you work all day and your needy Whippet will shiver away to nothing without human companionship. Most of the time, the breeder is only acting in the dog's best interest. She just may be saving you from lots of heartache and trouble. Rather than getting angry, talk frankly with the breeder about why she doesn't think you should own one of her puppies, and ask her what breed she thinks might suit your needs better. A boisterous Lab puppy loves to play with boisterous kids. A toy dog can get plenty of exercise indoors and doesn't necessarily need a fenced yard. A Basset Hound may be perfectly happy to snooze all day when you are at work, as long as you pay him lots of attention when you get home. Just because this particular breeder doesn't have a dog to suit your needs doesn't mean there isn't a perfect dog out there just waiting for you to find him.

- The breeder is already familiar with the different personalities and tendencies of the individual puppies in the litter.
- The breeder holds and plays with the puppies every day to help socialize them, starting soon after birth.
- The whelping area is clean and smells pleasant.
- The breeder is happy to introduce you to the mother of the litter and maybe even the father (although many sires don't live with the breeder).
- The mother of the litter is friendly and looks healthy.
- The puppies look plump and clean, with no crusted feces on their rears, no runny eyes or noses, no parasites, and no missing patches of hair. They are energetic and curious.

Good breeders will generally ask questions to gauge your suitability for their puppies.

- The breeder refuses to sell you a puppy younger than eight weeks old. (Some toy breeds shouldn't leave the whelping box until 12 weeks.)
- The breeder requires that you both sign a contract guaranteeing the puppy's health for a certain period of time under the condition that you take the puppy immediately to a vet for a checkup.

- The breeder's contract also requires you to promise you will return the dog to the breeder if you are ever unable to keep it, for any reason at any time (but not for a refund of money unless the reason for the return is the fault of the breeder, such as a serious genetic fault or contagious disease the puppy contracted while in the care of the breeder).
- The contract also requires that you neuter your pet, and the breeder requires proof that you have done so. If you buy a show dog and plan to exhibit your prized pet in the conformation show ring, the breeder will not require that you neuter your dog, as this would disqualify him from the ring. However, in this case, the breeder may require or request that any future mating be done under her guidance or may ask for the privilege of picking a puppy from any future litter.
- The breeder requests that you use her as a resource for information in the future (within reason—don't call her at all hours asking questions you can easily find answers to in dog care books or from your vet). Breeders can be an invaluable and lifelong source of information and guidance, and they usually love to keep in touch with their puppies as they grow.

How did your breeder do? Pretty well or not so well? If you have doubts about your breeder (or even if you don't think you have doubts), also see how your potential puppy's first human companion measures up against the "Not-So-Good Breeder" list.

The Not-So-Good Breeder List

You're not quite sure this breeder is breeding with

The mother of the litter should be healthy and friendly.

your puppy's good health and sound temperament in mind. Be sure—and run the other way fast without looking any further at the puppies—if the breeder you are visiting has any of the following qualities:

- First impressions first. The breeder is hurried, seems suspicious, acts like you are wasting her time, or doesn't give the impression of honesty. Use your instincts. If you don't feel like the breeder is trustworthy or you get the impression she is hiding something, thank her and move on.
- The breeder doesn't seem to know much about the breed or only tells you the good things. Every breed has its downside, and breeders who don't let you know the challenges may just be trying to make a quick buck. If you know more about the breed than the breeder, move on.
- The breeder breeds many different breeds and/or runs a huge breeding operation with many rows of kennels.
- The breeder is just breeding her first or second litter and doesn't know any of the experienced breeders in the business. Ask where she got the dam and sire and how she decided to start breeding. "I thought it would be fun" is not a good answer.

Good breeders can be a lifelong source of information and guidance.

- The breeder tells you that health tests in this breed aren't necessary or doesn't appear to know anything about health tests.
- The breeder is reluctant to give you the number of her vet and other references, or says she never takes her puppies to the vet because "they are so healthy."
- The breeder doesn't ask you anything about how you live, where you will keep the dog, or your dog experience. She seems more concerned with convincing you to buy a puppy, not with whether you would make a good guardian for this breed and this puppy.
- The breeder tries to get you to buy a puppy who is sick or shy.
- The breeder doesn't know anything about the individual puppies in the litter or says they are "all about the same."

> **Breeders should know a lot about their breed and provide information on the breed's positives and negatives.**

- The breeder doesn't frequently hold or play with or otherwise socialize the puppies, or doesn't seem to know anything about puppy socialization. (Ask what she does to socialize the puppies.)
- The whelping area is dirty and smells bad. Puppies defecate often, so an occasional pile or puddle is normal, but you should get the impression

the whelping area is cleaned and sterilized frequently (daily).

- The breeder makes excuses for why you can't see either of the parents of the litter.
- The breeder lets you see one or both parents of the litter, but the parents don't match the breed standard in some obvious way (much too big, too small, the wrong color, etc.), look unhealthy, or act very shy, aggressive, or unfriendly.
- The puppies look dirty or skinny, have dull coats, are crusted with feces or dirt, or have runny eyes, noses, or ears or missing patches of hair.
- The puppies have fleas or ticks.
- The puppies are shy, act sleepy all the time (every puppy has to sleep sometimes, but if you catch the litter sleeping, ask when you can come back to see them awake), seem low on energy, or are not curious at all to see you or explore their surroundings.

- The breeder is willing to sell you a puppy younger than eight weeks old.
- The breeder tries to give you a "deal" on a sick or low-energy puppy.
- The breeder doesn't require that you sign any kind of contract.

Rescue Me

The American Kennel Club (AKC) keeps a list of purebred dog rescue organizations by breed on its website. Check it out at akc.org/breeds/rescue.cfm.

- The breeder doesn't even mention spaying/neutering a pet.
- The breeder tells you or gives you the impression that once she has your money, you are on your own.
- The breeder has a health guarantee that covers the puppy only for a very short period of time, such as 36 hours, after which any further health problems, genetic or not, contracted from the breeder's facility or not, are your problem.
- You get a bad feeling—trust your instincts.

Let's hope the breeder you find with the puppy you love is a far cry from this last list. Either way, now you know what to expect, what to look for, and how to find a breeder who is doing everything she can to improve the breed and produce healthy, beautiful, and good-tempered puppies.

RESCUE DOGS

Maybe you are one of those people who, as much as you love dogs and appreciate the qualities of different breeds, don't feel the need to have a purebred dog. Maybe you'd rather rescue a mixed breed from the shelter. Or maybe you have a special affinity for a particular breed, but would rather rescue a dog who has lost his home than buy a puppy from a breeder. Good for you!

Rescue dogs can be the most rewarding of pets. Some people claim that dogs from animal shelters seem particularly grateful, as if they understand what you have done for them. Dogs from purebred rescue groups are often well trained and well behaved, but their owners simply couldn't

Breeder health guarantees should cover your puppy for genetic health problems.

keep them, or they have imperfect conformation but make perfect pets.

There are many other advantages to adopting a rescue dog:

- Puppies are difficult! Adult rescue dogs are usually past the young puppy stage, are already housetrained, and don't have to go out so often. They are past the teething, chewing, and play-biting stages. No puppy whining in the middle of the night, no puppy accidents, no puppy destruction.
- Rescue dogs are often already familiar with basic obedience commands like *sit*, *stay*, and *come*. It can be fun figuring out what your new dog already knows how to do.
- Rescue dogs older than age two or three (depending on the breed) are also past the trying stage of canine adolescence (can you say "teenager"?) and have already calmed down considerably.
- Many illnesses and genetic conditions will already have manifested by the time a dog becomes an adult, so if your rescue dog is healthy, he has a good chance of remaining healthy (provided you take good care of him).
- Rescue adult

Purebred rescue dogs are often well trained, well behaved, and grateful for your love.

dogs cost less initially, have usually already had all their initial puppy vaccinations, are probably already neutered, and don't require puppy supplies. Of course, they will still need regular veterinary checkups, a quality food, and other pet supplies.

- What you see is what you get. An older dog's looks and temperament are pretty much set, unlike with a puppy, where you can never be sure exactly how he will look or act as an adult.
- If you get a puppy from a shelter or rescue group—dogs often come in pregnant and give birth right there in the shelter, or a litter of puppies is abandoned—you can rescue a dog and still start from square one, socializing, training, and bonding with your puppy from the beginning.

Every animal shelter and every rescue group is different. Some have stringent requirements for adopters, such as requiring written permission from a landlord for renters or proof of home ownership, proof of a fence, and detailed personal interviews.

All of this fuss is important, even if you find it irritating. So many dogs are relinquished to shelters and rescue groups each year and so many dogs are returned to shelters

Older dogs have often already settled into their looks and temperament.

and rescue groups that these groups do everything their resources allow them to do in order to stop the cycle of abandonment for each dog they place. They want to be sure that every dog has a permanent, loving home. They love dogs and they don't want to see your pal back in the shelter again.

So take a deep breath, roll up your pant legs, and wade into the red tape. Your rescue dog will be well worth it. (I know mine was!)

SIGNS OF PUPPY HEALTH

Once you've secured a source for your new puppy, whether breeder, rescue group, or shelter, make sure that the pup you choose is as healthy as possible. How do you know? The most important thing for any new puppy owner to do is to take that new puppy immediately to the vet, even before you head home. Most breeders, shelters, and pet stores require or strongly recommend this practice, and if a vet finds a problem, you can take the puppy back before you ever get him home. (If you can bear it—some people would rather pay to fix the problem.) The worst-case scenario is a puppy with a serious contagious illness like parvo. In a

Shelters may have basic requirements for adopters to ensure that their dogs find permanent, loving homes.

few cases, puppies won't survive. The pet store, rescue group, shelter, or breeder must know when this happens, and should be willing to reimburse you for any expenses and for the price of the puppy if the problem was already present when you adopted your pup.

Your vet is the most qualified to assess your new puppy's health, but there are some general signs that a puppy is healthy and some signs that he isn't. Also look for signs that he has a good temperament. Take this list with you and assess your potential puppy for all of the following:

- How is his coat? A puppy's coat should be soft, shiny, unmatted, and clean. It shouldn't have any bare patches or look sparse, greasy, or otherwise unhealthy or unkempt.
- How is the skin beneath the coat? A puppy's skin should be free of red, itchy hot spots and dry flaky patches. Also check for signs of fleas—little black specks of flea dirt or the tiny brown, hopping fleas themselves—and ticks, which can be the size of a pinhead or swollen up to the size of a large beetle, crawling or attached to the skin. Healthy puppy skin should be soft and pinkish.
- Is your puppy clean? He

Bring your new puppy to the veterinarian immediately after leaving the breeder, rescue group, or shelter.

should not smell foul and should not have any crusted feces, dirt, or discharge from any orifice.

- Are his eyes bright and shiny without being runny? Is his expression alert?
- Is he energetic and curious? Does he climb around exploring, playing with littermates, nuzzling mom, or checking you out? Be wary of puppies who are too shy, don't seem to have any energy or curiosity, or are overly boisterous and aggressive compared to littermates.
- Are his ears clean?
- Are his teeth white and sharp? (He may not have all his teeth yet, depending on how old he is when you are first introduced.)

- Is his nose soft and wet without being runny?
- Are his paws clean and his paw pads soft (not cracked, covered in sores, or dirty)?
- Is he interested in you? Does he display affection to you? A playful spirit?

If your puppy checks out, let the vet do a more thorough checkup. Once you've got the green light from your vet, you can take that puppy home and begin some serious bonding.

VETERINARY CARE

Your vet is one of the most important allies in your quest to give your new dog a healthy life. She should see your new puppy several times during the first year for vaccinations and checkups and can also serve as a resource for information about diet, pest control, grooming, potential emergencies ("My puppy just ate a button—is it an emergency?"), and even basic behavioral modification and training.

But just as it is with medical doctors for humans, some vets have a great rapport with pets and humans alike, and some, even if they are very skilled, may not make you feel comfortable. Having a good relationship with your vet is important. Ideally, you and your vet will understand each other and share a similar philosophy of pet care, whether that means integrating holistic and/ or preventive health care measures, sticking to conventional care only, or doing as much as possible on your own at home. When you and your vet are on the same page, everybody wins.

Choosing a Vet

Choosing a vet is as important as choosing a doctor. In fact, it *is* choosing a doctor! Depending on where you live, you may have many choices or just a few, but being choosy in the beginning can pay off later. (And if your veterinarian doesn't work out, you can always switch vets.)

Schedule appointments to meet a few vets in your area, either just to talk or to have your dog generally checked over for good health. While you are

Thoroughly research your options when choosing your veterinarian.

Don't Forget the Annual Checkup

After that first year, you may believe that your bouncing adolescent is the picture of perfect health, but don't neglect an annual checkup. The annual exam gives your vet a chance to monitor your dog and could catch a problem while it is still treatable and before it gets too serious. Of course, if your pet's behavior or habits suddenly change, or if he develops any lumps, bumps, sores, or injuries between annual exams, take him to the vet immediately.

there, pay attention and ask questions. Here's what to look for and what to ask:

First impressions can be helpful when choosing your veterinarian.

- Is the vet easily accessible? A better vet may be worth a longer drive, but if the vet is too far away and you have an emergency, you may not be able to get there in time. Ask if there is an alternate location for an emergency clinic.
- Is it easy to make an appointment when you call ahead? Is the receptionist friendly? Will they let you meet the vet and/or schedule a physical for your dog without extra tests? A vet with no time to

meet and spend time with potential clients may be too busy when you need her most. On the other hand, a busy vet can be a sign of a quality vet because word gets around.

- What is your first impression of the reception area? Is it clean and does it smell pleasant? Is the staff friendly and welcoming? Do you feel comfortable there? Bad smells, harried staff, and dirty facilities are all bad signs. Worried animals in the waiting room are, of course, a fixture at any vet.
- Do you have to wait more than 15 minutes, and if you do, are you told that this is due to unusual circumstances? You and your pet shouldn't be kept waiting for too long. Sure, the vet is busy, but so are you. You don't want a vet who overschedules on purpose.
- Is the office a large multi-vet practice or a small in-home operation? Which environment do you prefer? Which makes you feel more comfortable?
- When you are shown into the waiting room, are you made to feel comfortable?
- Does the staff seem competent? Do they weigh your dog, get him ready, and behave in a professional way that keeps your dog as calm as possible?
- How does the vet treat you? How does the vet treat your dog? Does she have a friendly, open personality, or does she seem

disinclined to talk to you? Does she act like she likes animals, or does she act like she's burned out and could care less if she ever sees another puppy? Does she act like she loves dogs but can't stand people? A good vet should be able to relate well and communicate well with both you and your dog.

- After all is said and done, how are the prices? Call around to see if they are comparable to other vets in the area. Prices for veterinary services vary widely according to geographical location, so a vet in

Fearless Fido?

Your first impression and intuition about a vet can tell you a lot about whether that person will be a good vet for you and your dog. However, don't necessarily take your dog's cue. Many pets are frightened at any veterinarian office, especially those who have had previous unpleasant experiences there (and what puppy enjoys those vaccinations?) and those who are intimidated or riled up by other pets in the waiting room. A frightened puppy isn't necessarily telling you he doesn't like the vet. On the other hand, if you know your dog well and you know he is usually fine with vets but acts strange, either fearful or aggressive, with a particular vet, consider that a red flag.

Manhattan will probably charge much more than a vet in rural Iowa.

First Exam

Whether you are still trying out potential vets or have secured one you love, your new puppy must visit the vet right away, preferably on the way home from the breeder, animal shelter, or pet store. At this very first exam, you can expect the vet to do certain things. Although some vets vary according to what they believe is necessary, most vets will begin by checking your new puppy out carefully for genetic defects in structure. The vet will look at and palpate (feel) your puppy's head, ears, eyes, nose, mouth, jaw, neck, spine, legs, tail, genitalia, ribs, and coat for lumps, bumps, or anything malformed. Your vet isn't looking for things that would disqualify a puppy from the show ring, just things that would compromise his health, such as malformed bones, teeth, eyes, or paws; parasites like fleas and ticks; signs of other skin problems such as allergies or fungus; as well as other signs of disease.

If your puppy hasn't yet had his first vaccinations, the vet will administer

Good veterinarians should relate and communicate well with both you and your dog.

those, along with a worming, for which you will need a fresh stool sample, so come prepared. (See the list provided below.)

Many vets will also be willing to answer any questions you have about puppy care and may advise you on when to have your pet neutered.

Don't come to that first vet visit empty-handed. Be sure to bring:

- Your puppy's vaccination history, if he has one.
- Copies of all records of previous medical care for your puppy's file. (Keep your own copies at home in a safe place, too.) If you bought your puppy from a breeder, the breeder should provide you with this information.
- If your puppy is on any medications, even an over-the-counter cream or pet vitamins, bring those in to show your vet.
- That fresh stool sample—collect your puppy's most recent in a plastic bag and keep it in the refrigerator until it's time to go to the vet. (You may want to double bag it.)
- A list of any questions you will want to remember to ask.

WHY SPAY OR NEUTER?

The benefits of having your pet spayed or neutered are numerous. Spayed females tend to live longer

Bring your puppy's vaccination history, medical records, medication schedule, and stool sample (along with your questions!) to his first veterinary examination.

Early Spaying or Neutering

Some vets and animal shelters recommend that puppies be neutered much earlier than once recommended, because of the benefits to the pets and the owners, and to help stem the pet overpopulation problem. Other benefits are that younger animals tolerate anesthesia better and may recover faster. The traditional age for neutering is between six and seven months of age, but some puppies are now neutered as young as six or seven weeks old. This is controversial, however. There is some evidence that early spaying or neutering can decrease performance in canine athletes and may put dogs at greater risk for some serious health issues, including orthopedic problems and several types of cancer. Some veterinarians even suggest waiting longer, even up to a year, before spaying or neutering. Talk to your veterinarian about the best time to spay or neuter your dog, or stay on the safe side and wait until the second half of your puppy's first year.

and be healthier in general. You won't have to deal with messy heat cycles (think canine sanitary diapers or blood spots on the floor), and you won't risk an unwanted litter of puppies. If you spay your female dog before her first heat cycle, you will greatly reduce the risk of mammary, ovarian, and uterine cancers.

Neutering a male dog can result in a calmer animal with less aggression towards other dogs. Your male dog won't try to escape when he senses a female in heat and may be better behaved in general. He may urine-mark in the house less often and may be less likely to "hump" legs, chairs, and other dogs (so embarrassing!). Neutered males can't get testicular cancer, since they have no testicles. They are also less likely to have prostate problems as they age.

VACCINATIONS

When a puppy is nursing, he receives antibodies against disease from his mother's milk (just like a human baby does). Once he stops nursing, however, that protection quickly fades, leaving a new puppy vulnerable to disease. For this reason, newly weaned puppies must begin a vaccination schedule.

Common Diseases to Vaccinate Against

Vaccinations are very important for puppies, as all dogs are at risk for contracting very serious, even fatal diseases that vaccination can prevent. The most dangerous of these include:

- **Canine adenovirus:** This contagious virus causes upper respiratory tract infection and can also damage the liver, kidneys, and eyes. It starts in the throat and then moves into the organs. There are various levels or stages of the disease, some more severe than others. It's better to avoid it completely through vaccination.

- **Canine distemper:** This serious and contagious virus is incurable. It used to be a leading cause of death in dogs but is now almost eliminated because of vaccinations. Initial signs include fever, red eyes, and nasal and eye discharge. Later signs include lethargy, vomiting or diarrhea, refusal to eat, and eventually seizures, paralysis, and sometimes death.

- **Canine parvovirus:** Another highly contagious virus, this one still poses a problem in some areas. There are two forms of the disease—an intestinal form, which causes vomiting, diarrhea, and refusal to eat, and a rarer cardiac form, which targets the heart muscle and is usually fatal. Fortunately, vaccination has reduced incidence of this disease, but puppies can still die from it. Vaccination is essential!

- **Rabies:** Another disease that used to kill a lot of dogs, rabies is now much rarer due to vaccinations. Rabies is the only vaccination required by law because this very serious and sometimes fatal disease can be spread to humans. In dogs, rabies

When puppies are nursing, they receive antibodies against disease from their mother's milk.

is nearly always fatal. It affects the brain and central nervous system and is usually contracted through the bite of a wild animal. Symptoms include fever, seizures, paralysis, refusal to drink water, sudden aggression, stumbling and lack of coordination, jaw or throat paralysis, and drooling.

Other diseases that your puppy may be vaccinated for include:

• **Bordetella (kennel cough):** Bordetella causes a cough and is similar to bronchitis in humans. It is caused by bacteria and is highly contagious.
• **Canine influenza:** The canine version of the flu, this contagious virus also causes respiratory distress.

Signs include coughing, a runny nose, and fever. The infection can become serious in some dogs, but is rarely fatal.

Vaccination protocols are updated every few years.

• **Canine parainfluenza:** This contagious virus affects the respiratory system and causes coughing. Signs include a dry or moist cough, mild fever, runny nose, and lack of energy.
• **Leptospirosis:** This bacterial disease can also affect both dogs and people. Signs include fever, muscle stiffness and pain, shivering, weakness, increased thirst and

urination, dehydration, refusal to eat, diarrhea, yellow skin and eyes, coughing, increased respiration, a runny nose, and lymph-node swelling. The infection usually occurs through contact with wet environments, like wetlands or flood waters, or in subtropical or tropical climates.

- **Lyme disease:** The most common tick-transmitted disease in the world, Lyme disease occurs when a tick bites a dog (or human) and transmits a specific bacterium. Signs include lameness due to joint inflammation, walking stiffly or with an arched back, sensitivity, breathing issues, fever, and swollen lymph nodes near the tick bite. Sometimes depression and loss of appetite can occur. In serious cases, the kidneys or other vital organs can be affected. Humans can get Lyme disease from ticks that come in on their dogs, but it is only transmitted by the very small (and hard-to-spot) deer tick, which must be attached for at least 18 hours in order to transmit the bacteria.

Basic Vaccination Schedule

In the past, dogs may have been vaccinated more than necessary because there were no official guidelines for vaccinations other than those published by vaccine manufacturers. That all changed in 2003 when the American Animal Hospital Association (AAHA) published its first canine vaccine guidelines. These are reviewed and updated every few years and seek to strike a balance between vaccination for genuine pet safety and overvaccination, which can put some sensitive animals at risk for reactions.

The guidelines recommend a set of core vaccinations for every dog and additional vaccinations that veterinarians can use with discretion, according to an individual dog's risk of contracting a particular disease. For

Puppy-proofing your home means protecting both home and puppy!

example, an outdoorsy dog in a tick-prone area may benefit from the Lyme disease vaccine, but a city dog living in an apartment may not.

A basic core vaccination schedule includes shots for canine distemper, canine parvovirus, canine adenovirus, and rabies. Starting when your puppy is six weeks old, he would be vaccinated for the first three illnesses every three to four weeks, the last vaccination occurring between weeks 14 and 16. He would receive a booster shot one year after the last initial dose and be revaccinated every three years after that—or less often, as recommended by your doctor. For rabies, your puppy would be vaccinated once at 12 weeks or later, as required by law, and revaccinated as required by law. (This may be annually or less often, such as every three years.)

Some vets suggest schedules slightly different from this one, and you should follow your vet's recommendation for your individual dog.

Noncore vaccinations can be given according to owner and veterinary discretion. These include vaccinations for canine parainfluenza, bordetella, canine influenza, Lyme disease, and leptospirosis. Talk to your veterinarian about whether any of these vaccinations are recommended for your dog.

PUPPY-PROOFING YOUR HOME

Another health-related step before you bring your new puppy into your home is to puppy-proof the house. Puppies are curious, quick, able to squirm into spaces you wouldn't believe, and they can get into a lot of trouble . . . fast.

The problem is that you never know just what a puppy is going to do until he does it. Oops, there goes your new sock. Oops, apparently your puppy enjoys tug of war with the drapes. Oops, wasn't there a chicken on the table a few minutes ago, and where *is* that dog? The best way to make at least a fair guess about what your puppy might get into is to spend some time around your house at puppy level. Yes, that means down on the floor, about a foot (0.3 m) off the ground. Look around—what do you see?

Think about what looks tempting

Puppy Poison Control

What if your puppy licked up some tasty but highly toxic antifreeze from the garage? What if he got into some really rotten garbage? Did you know acetaminophen could kill your puppy and so could chocolate? Keep the ASPCA Animal Poison Control hotline number handy at all times: 888-426-4435. Its website also has lots of information about pet safety: aspca.org/pet-care/animal-poison-control. If you call the hotline, you will be charged a consulting fee to talk to a vet, but the fee is well worth a dog's life.

to chew or play with. Remember that puppies explore with their mouths, so small objects—paper clips, stray buttons, little plastic toys—can be choking hazards, and garbage, plants, medications, and household chemicals can be poisonous. Keep the floor picked up and vacuumed.

Make sure your puppy has access to lots of chew toys so that whenever he zeroes in on something you don't want him to chew, you can quickly replace it with something he is allowed to chew. Soon he will learn to choose his own toys instead of your shoes.

Also make sure to keep garbage and houseplants inaccessible and keep medication, household cleaners, and other chemicals out of reach, including chemicals stored under sinks, in basements and garages, and in sheds. Automobile and lawn and garden products can be particularly hazardous outside, where we may not realize how accessible they are.

Once your home is neat, safe, and sound, make sure your puppy has a special spot for eating, a special spot for sleeping undisturbed, and lots of attention and supervision during those first months as he learns the

Give your puppy special spots for eating and sleeping undisturbed, along with plenty of supervision and love.

house rules and you get to know each other better. Keep your puppy safe and the two of you may enjoy many happy years together.

YOUR CANINE–HUMAN RELATIONSHIP

Living with a dog is more than a matter of sharing your living space. Dogs are social animals, and because they have been bred for centuries not only to live with but also to work and interact with humans, dogs are hardwired to need us. Sure, wild dogs can live without humans, but the domestic dogs we know and love won't be able to fulfill their potential without the partnership of people. No matter how smart your dog is, if you don't help to give him outlets to exercise his intelligence, you may never find out.

One of the best things about living with a dog is the dog–human relationship, but this relationship is also one of the easiest things to miss or ruin through bad management. Dog ownership entails getting to

Don't let a day go by without spending some serious one-on-one time with your dog.

know this member of another species and becoming friends.

You have many different ways to build a strong and healthy relationship with your puppy. Training, playing, or simply spending time with your puppy will all help your relationship. Miscommunication, anger, hitting, and ignoring him will quickly destroy that relationship.

Here are some ideas for building your canine–human bond.

One-on-One Time

Don't let a day go by without spending some serious one-on-one time with your puppy. In this case, quality counts for more than quantity. If you take just 15 minutes out of your day to pay attention to your dog and nothing else, you'll both feel closer and the bonding will go a long way toward making your dog feel like he is getting enough attention, which can allay all kinds of behavioral problems, like nervous chewing, digging, and chronic barking. Puppies often misbehave because they aren't getting enough human interaction, so make sure you interact with your dog in a positive way.

Spend your bonding time petting, talking to, or playing with your puppy.

Tap into your dog's natural sense of play and the two of you will have a great time together.

Turn off the TV if it distracts you from your buddy, and don't talk on the phone. Don't keep leaving to tend to the kids or other things, and don't make the time about rigorous training. Make it positive, fun, and preferably calm so that your puppy associates time with you with a feeling of tranquility rather than hyperactivity. Lots of quiet, relaxed stroking and murmurs of "good puppy" are nice. Some gentle games can be fun, too. No tug-of-war, but perhaps some retrieving or running around together in the yard followed by some downtime.

Three 5-minute sessions at different times during the day work just as well as one 15-minute block.

Just about anything can become a toy or game for your puppy.

Playtime

Puppies love to play (and older dogs enjoy it, too). If you are playful with your puppy instead of impatient, both of you will enjoy your time together much more. Throw a ball or a stick. Play gentle tug-of-war with small dogs. (Tug-of-war games can encourage larger dogs, especially guardian breeds, to be too aggressive.) Chase your dog around the yard or practice tricks you've taught him. Go to the dog park or for a walk around the block or go exploring in a nearby natural area.

Life is full of interesting smells and sounds. Just about anything can become a toy or be made into a game. Tap into your dog's natural sense of play and the two of you will have a great time together. You'll both have a whole lot of fun and a stronger relationship, too.

Exercise

Puppies have a natural instinct to play. Playing with littermates teaches puppies about social interaction, and it also exercises those puppy muscles. When puppies are tiny, it's easy for them to get enough exercise, but when you bring a puppy home, you have to pick up where those littermates left off.

Exercise is just as important for dogs as it is for humans, and for all the same reasons. Exercise keeps excess weight off a dog. It keeps the heart in good working order. It keeps the joints limber and healthy. It also contributes to a positive, relaxed mental state. Regular exercise is one of the greatest gifts you can give your dog.

Obesity is incredibly common in pet dogs. Vets

> **Exercise keeps a puppy at a healthy weight and contributes to a relaxed mental state.**

often express to me their concern that obesity is the most common problem among the pets they see in their offices. Except for rare cases that involve medical problems, dogs become obese for two reasons: They eat too much and don't exercise enough.

A puppy's youth has four stages: early puppyhood (birth to six months), late puppyhood (six months to one year), adolescence (one to two or three years, depending on the breed), and young adulthood (two to three years to five to seven years, depending on the breed). Each of these stages has different exercise requirements and challenges you must help your puppy meet so that he can enjoy a healthy, active life.

Exercise for Young Puppies: Damage Control

In early puppyhood, dogs naturally take care of their own exercise needs until they leave the whelping box. When you take your new puppy home, he will have a lot of energy. No, I mean a *lot* of energy. In fact, one of the

> A tired puppy is a well-behaved puppy, as dog trainers like to say.

biggest challenges of new puppies (beyond housetraining) is keeping up with all that energy, something many people find too challenging because they aren't prepared for it.

Puppies without outlets for their high-intensity energy often turn to destruction, and depending on your puppy's breed, that destruction can be pretty major. Consider the pair of female Bloodhound puppies who ate through their family's living room wall all the way to the dining room, right through the sheet rock, when they were left alone. Or what about the Afghan who ate the dashboard out of the car in which his human left him? Or the Golden Retriever–Shar-Pei mix who ate the molding from around the front door when his human companion went to work? New puppy owners lose shoes, clothing, underwear, even whole pieces of furniture—couches with juicy cushions; dining room chairs with nice, chewable legs; feather pillows too tempting not to gut and spread around the room with puppy abandon.

Young puppies need lots of playtime that stimulates them both physically and mentally. They need lots of activity with you to keep them busy. They need chew toys and they need to be taught what is and what is not acceptable for chewing. They also require leash training so that they can eventually safely accompany you outside the perimeter of your fence.

If you set aside time every day in the morning and evening to exercise your young puppy, you'll also be exercising damage control. A tired puppy is a well-behaved puppy, as dog trainers like to say.

One of the biggest challenges of owning a puppy is their high energy level.

7

GREAT HEALTH: YEAR ONE AND BEYOND

After the first year, your puppy will grow into a dog, and your relationship will continue to grow, too. Of course, this is still a time to practice regular health care, keep up with veterinary checkups, and continue with training and grooming. You might transition your dog's diet after the first year, and you will want to keep fostering a healthy relationship. That means doing things together, getting exercise every day, and staying tuned-in to make sure your dog is healthy.

THE HEALTHY DOG

A healthy dog has a shiny coat, bright eyes, a moist nose, sharp white teeth, smooth and supple skin, flexible paw pads, and short nails. A healthy dog feels good, is free from pain, can move easily and freely, has enough energy to play and exercise, eats well, sleeps well, and enjoys human company. A well-bred, well-cared-for dog who gets regular exercise, eats a balanced, high-quality diet, and receives regular veterinary care, socialization, training, and bonding time with humans will likely be healthy for most of his life. Chances are your dog will be just fine for most of his life. However, dogs, just like people, can develop many different kinds of health

> Knowing the signs that could indicate a health problem could save your dog's life.

problems. Most are mild and easy to resolve. Some are more serious. It's better to know the signs and what to do, just in case. With most medical issues, from fleas to cancer, the sooner your dog gets treatment, the better the outcome.

What can you do to keep your dog as healthy as he can be for as long as possible? Several very important things:

- Pay attention. The weekly grooming exam and time spent with your dog each day will help you to monitor his health.
- Schedule an annual exam. Your vet is trained to detect problems you may not notice and will also do standard tests to make sure your dog is healthy.
- Keep up on first-year vaccinations to prevent infectious diseases.
- Supervise your dog and don't let him roam loose where he could pick up diseases and/or become injured.

Signs Something Could Be Wrong

If you pay attention to your dog's behavior, eating and drinking habits, skin, coat, eyes, ears, nose, mouth, and paws, you will notice when something changes. A change in habits or in your dog's body should always put

you on the alert. However, you can keep an eye out for some specific things that could signal a health problem. Almost every section in this chapter will have an alert list, but some of the general signs of a health problem include the following and are worth a call to the vet:

- acting uncharacteristically nervous, jumpy, or depressed
- any lumps, bumps, itching, or irritated skin patches
- cracked paw pads
- discharge from nose
- disorientation
- displays uncharacteristically low energy
- doesn't seem to hear
- doesn't seem to see well, bumps into things

A healthy dog has a shiny coat and bright eyes.

- ear shaking or scratching
- hair loss
- limping or favoring a leg
- noticeable plaque on teeth
- red, irritated, or receding gums
- red, swollen, or runny eyes
- sleeping more than normal, especially lasting more than a day or two
- sudden inability to jump up or down from couches, beds, etc.
- suddenly moving more slowly
- sudden noticeable increase in thirst (drinking water more often)
- sudden noticeable increase or decrease in appetite, especially lasting more than a day or two
- sudden refusal to be active, run, or jump
- sudden reluctance to climb stairs
- uncharacteristic irritability or lethargy
- yelping in pain when touched

Again, any of these symptoms could have simple explanations and easy solutions, but they could also indicate more serious health problems, so please don't ignore changes in

Contact your veterinarian if your dog exhibits behavioral or physical changes such as ear scratching, disorientation, or hair loss.

your pet. Stay in contact with your vet, your best ally in the quest to keep your dog healthy and happy.

Liquids, Injections, and Suppositories

If your dog's medication isn't in pill form, it will be in the form of a liquid to be swallowed or injected or in suppository form. Your vet can show you how to administer all these forms of medication, but liquids and suppositories are usually easy to give your dog.

To administer liquid medicine from a syringe, hold your dog's head around the ears, pull back the side of his mouth, insert the syringe (or eyedropper) into the cheek pouch, hold his lips around the syringe so that medicine can't leak out, tilt your dog's head back, and dispense the medicine. Your dog should swallow automatically.

Your dog may need a suppository if he is unable to keep pills or liquid in his stomach due to vomiting. A suppository must be lubricated with petroleum jelly and inserted into the anal canal.

To give your dog an injection, such as in the case of a severe allergic reaction or if your pet is diabetic and requires insulin, have your vet

> **Warning signs for health problems may have simple explanations and easy solutions or may require further attention.**

Give a Dog a Pill

If you find that your dog does have a health condition, you may need to give him medication that is prescribed by or recommended by your vet, and chances are, that medication will be in pill form.

Some dogs are happy to swallow a pill buried in a bit of cheese, meat paste (like liverwurst), canned dog food, or peanut butter. Others will find that pill, no matter how small, and spit it right back out. Always watch your dog if you give him a pill with food to be absolutely sure he swallows it. If he won't, you'll have to make sure the pill gets down that throat. Here's how.

1. Call your dog to you and hold his collar gently. Reassure him and calm him with gentle words and petting. If your dog is nervous or resistant, you may need another pair of hands to help hold and calm him.

2. With one hand, place your thumb right behind one of your dog's canine teeth (the long sharp ones on the top to the side), which will cause him to open his mouth.

3. Holding the pill or capsule with your other hand, use that hand to push your dog's lower jaw down. Place the pill as far back as you can on the middle of your dog's tongue. If you put it to the side, your dog can spit it out easily.

4. Close your dog's mouth and massage his throat until he swallows.

5. When your dog licks his nose, you will know he has swallowed the pill.

demonstrate the correct method. Injections are either subcutaneous, which means they are administered just under the skin and typically are not painful, or intramuscular, which means they must be injected directly into the muscle. Your dog may find these momentarily painful, and you may need someone to help you hold your dog.

How to Take a Dog's Temperature

A dog's normal temperature averages 101.3°F (38.5°C) but can range from 100° to 102.5°F (37.8°–39.2°C). A newborn puppy's temperature is between 94° and 97°F (34.4°–36.1°C) at birth and reaches an average of 100°F (37.8°C) by four weeks.

You probably won't ever need to take your dog's temperature, but if you suspect your dog is sick and you want more information, use a digital thermometer specifically made for pets. Obviously, your dog isn't going to hold a thermometer in his mouth, so you're going to have to deal with the opposite end of your dog—you must take a rectal temperature.

Rub the end of the thermometer with a little petroleum jelly. Hold up your dog's tail, which will keep him in a standing position, and insert the thermometer with a twisting motion 1 to 3 inches (2.5–7.5 cm) into the anal canal (farther in for larger dogs). Hold the thermometer in place for three minutes, or in the case of a digital thermometer, until it beeps indicating it is finished. Read the thermometer, then clean it with alcohol.

R&R for Dogs

Some conditions, such as spinal disc ruptures, require enforced rest. Sometimes called crate rest, this treatment depends on your dog keeping still so that he can heal, sometimes for days at a time. This is a common treatment for Dachshunds and other long-backed dogs with canine intervertebral disc disease. Your dog must be confined to his crate except for bathroom breaks and encouraged to stay still and rest.

Canine medication comes in various forms.

While a sick dog probably won't want to move around much, once pain medications kick in and your dog starts to feel better, he will probably be itching to get out and play. He may whine, cry, beg, plead, and gaze at you with such a pathetic expression that you may be tempted to give in and let him out for just a little while.

Please follow your doctor's orders when it comes to crate rest. It could mean the difference between a future of normal function and a future of rear-leg paralysis for your dog. Remember who's the boss and don't let that wily puppy convince you otherwise.

PEST CONTROL

Most pet owners have had at least some experience with fleas. People who take their pets into wooded areas have probably also seen a tick or two. Pests like heartworms borne through the bite of a mosquito, tapeworms borne through the bite of a flea, and various kinds of mites may go unnoticed until serious symptoms emerge, making prevention crucial.

Probably the most common pests that pet owners must contend with are fleas, so let's look first at how to control fleas and all the problems they can cause for you and your pet.

A dog's normal temperature averages 101.3°F (38.5°C).

Fleas

Fleas are ubiquitous. Almost any dog who spends time outside in warm weather, especially around other dogs, will probably get a flea bite or two. In many cases, because fleas are opportunistic feeders and breeders, a few fleas will quickly become an infestation. You can tell if your pet has fleas by using a flea comb or your fingers to examine his skin, especially around the ears, underside, and groin area. Fleas are tiny brown insects; they crawl or jump and are difficult to catch, and even more difficult to crush between your fingers. If you remove them mechanically from your pet with a flea comb, drop them in rubbing alcohol to kill them, then flush them down the toilet.

Even if you don't see fleas, you may see flea dirt (little brownish-red specks of digested blood) and flea eggs (little white specks). Both are indicators that fleas are crawling around somewhere.

Fleas bite your dog to feed on blood. In a pinch, they may even bite you. Flea bites itch, and some dogs who are allergic to flea saliva can develop a condition called flea bite dermatitis, which causes severe itching and red, raw spots. Fleas can also transmit tapeworms to your dog.

Do Dogs Suffer From Stress?

Dogs—like any animal—can suffer from stress. Dogs are creatures of habit with a strong survival instinct and become agitated when their routines are broken or when they think they are in danger. This natural survival mechanism results in certain physiological changes: increased heart rate, blood pressure, and respiratory rate; adrenaline surges; and blood pumping to muscles and away from the digestive system. Too much agitation over a long period can result in chronic stress. Your dog's body isn't designed to undergo the physiological stress state very often, as this is meant for emergencies. Maybe your routine has changed. You moved to a new home, got a new job, had a baby, adopted a cat. Or maybe you've found a stray who has been living a stressful or possibly abusive existence. Patience, understanding, and a calming environment with good health care, sound nutrition, exercise, and plenty of love should eventually bring your stressed-out pet back to normal. Talk to your vet if your pet seems to be suffering from extreme anxiety or depression, or if you have found a stray dog who is very agitated, shy, aggressive, or fearful. Such behavior could also be the result of a physical problem. Anxious behavior can result in physical problems, and physical problems can result in anxious behavior, but rather than play "which came first," have your pet treated by a professional.

The most common flea to bite pet dogs is actually called the cat flea, or *Ctenocephalides felis*. At any time, only about one percent of the fleas in an environment (like your home) will be in adult form. The rest will be in egg, larval, or pupal form in carpets, furniture, and grass. That means getting rid of fleas is usually a multi-step process.

Fortunately, science has provided pet owners with an alternative to the messy and often toxic sprays, foggers, and collars once required for flea control. Topical spot-on products are liquids contained in one-application tubes that are applied to the skin between your dog's shoulder blades, and in the case of large dogs, at the base of the tail. These products move along the skin, kill adult fleas on contact within 12 to 24 hours, and are nontoxic because they don't enter your dog's bloodstream. Spot-ons are available through your veterinarian or pet stores and should be applied monthly during flea season. (In some areas, such as the South and Southwest, flea season can be all year long.) Follow product directions carefully.

Check your dog for fleas and ticks after he's been playing outdoors.

For mild infestations, spot-ons used monthly, along with a thorough weekly vacuuming of your carpets and upholstery and hot-water wash of all human and dog bedding, may be enough. As the remaining flea eggs hatch and the larvae develop and eventually become adult fleas, they will be killed when they jump on your dog.

Severe infestations may require a more complete approach: a flea dip or bath with flea shampoo, application of a spot-on, and a spray for carpets, furniture, and yards containing an adulticide to kill adult fleas as well as an insect growth regulator (IGR) to keep flea eggs from hatching. Vigilance all summer long, including weekly or even more frequent laundering of bedding and vacuuming of carpets and soft furniture, should keep fleas under control.

Topical spot-on products can be effective for preventing fleas.

Ticks

Ticks are also common in most areas of the US, although the variety of tick differs according to geographical location. Ticks can cause serious diseases, such as Lyme disease and Rocky Mountain spotted fever, in your dog (and in you). Ticks can attach to your dog anywhere but are common around the ears, feet, and belly. After your dog has spent time in any wooded area (even a residential yard with large trees), examine him (and yourself) for ticks.

Ticks feed on blood by inserting their heads under the skin. As they drink, their bodies swell, and once they are engorged, they drop off. *Never touch a tick with your bare hands.* A tick filled with blood can easily burst, getting infected fluid on your skin, which could infect you—

Caution for Cats

Some chemicals used in flea products for dogs are very toxic to cats. Never use a flea control product designed for dogs on a cat. Dog and cat flea control products are not interchangeable! Always follow package directions for any flea control product to prevent toxicity for your pet and for you.

tick in this way, never grab the body—which could make the tick regurgitate infected blood that might not have otherwise been transmitted—and use tweezers or a tool specifically made to pull out ticks. Your pet store likely has some options. Never try to burn or smother a tick, and remember, never touch a tick with your bare fingers. If a tick bite looks infected after you have removed the tick, talk to your veterinarian.

KEEPING A HEALTHY COAT

The pests listed in this section and their secondary conditions such as skin infections and allergic reactions are a major cause of skin and coat problems in dogs, but dogs can suffer from other skin and coat disorders, too. Canine skin is thinner than human skin, and if it is damaged, it can quickly become susceptible to infection.

The best way to keep your dog's skin and coat healthy is to keep him well-groomed with frequent brushing and not-too-frequent shampooing, so the skin's natural oils can keep the skin supple and coat shiny and resilient. Also, your dog should be on a high-quality food that doesn't cause an allergic reaction (your vet can test for food allergies) and which

Ticks can cause serious diseases, such as Lyme disease and Rocky Mountain spotted fever.

so always wear rubber gloves when handling ticks. If you find a tick crawling on your dog, immediately remove it with a tweezers or with a paper towel and drop it in rubbing alcohol to kill it. Then flush it down the toilet.

If a tick is attached, soak a cotton ball with rubbing alcohol, nail polish remover, or a product designed to kill ticks and apply it to the tick until it removes its head. You can then pull it off and drop it in alcohol to kill it. You can also grab an attached tick by the head and pull it straight out in one quick motion (without twisting, so the head doesn't break off and stay under the skin). When removing a contains enough essential fatty acids to keep skin in good condition. Keeping your dog's coat free of tangles and mats is also essential, since a matted coat can attract dirt and parasites, contributing to skin problems.

Catching any skin or coat changes early can help your vet diagnose and treat skin problems and diseases, of which there are many. Skin diseases come in different forms: Some result in severe itching, like flea bite dermatitis, flea allergy dermatitis, and other skin conditions caused by pests; food allergies can also cause dermatitis. Skin irritation sometimes arises due to contact with an irritant, and hormone disorders and genetic disorders can cause hair loss. Some conditions become infections with swelling, redness, and discharge. Other conditions are the result of immune-related or autoimmune-related conditions, and some are related to tumors, cysts, nodules, ulcers, and abscesses.

Alert your vet if you notice any of the following skin conditions

The best way to keep your dog's skin and coat healthy is to keep him well-groomed.

Pests and How to Treat Them

Pest	Symptoms	Dangers
Cheyletiella mange mites (walking dandruff): Most common in puppies from pet shops and kennels	Red bumpy rash, large flakes of dandruff in young puppies	Very contagious, can transmit to humans
Demodectic mange mites: Occur mainly in puppies and debilitated dogs	Patchy hair loss, scales, draining and crusty sores	Can result in skin infections and may permanently compromise skin and hair coat; may be genetic, so affected dogs shouldn't be bred
Ear mites	Itching and scratching of ears, violent head shaking	Highly contagious, though not to humans; can cause bacterial infections
Flies and maggots: Injured or ill strays or severely neglected dogs are most at risk	Maggots infest and infect open wounds and mats in coat on old, sick, or weak dogs	Severe bacterial infection can cause shock and even death
Heartworms: Most at risk are dogs who spend more time outdoors and those living in southeastern Atlantic and Gulf Coast regions	Can cause fatigue, cough, weight loss, rapid breathing, fainting, bulging chest, and death	Loss of health and eventually, death
Intestinal worms (such as ascarids, hookworms, roundworms, tapeworms, threadworms, whipworms): Many dogs have them and their systems keep them in check, but immune-suppressed and stressed dogs may develop an infection	Diarrhea, anemia, weight loss, blood in feces	Some intestinal worms can also infect humans and can cause serious diseases; children often affected by eating dirt or sand in feces-soiled environment
Protozoan diseases: Such as giardiasis, trichomoniasis, and coccidiosis	Diarrhea, sometimes bloody	Giardiasis could be transmitted to humans, probably through infected water supply
Ringworm: Not actually a parasite, though often mistaken for one, ringworm is a fungus that affects hair follicles	Hair loss in a circular pattern surrounded by a red ring and containing a scaly center	Can result in a bacterial skin infection; often transmitted to humans, frequently to children, through contact
Scabies mites (sarcoptic mange)	Severe itching, rash, hair loss, crusty ear tips	Very contagious, extreme scratching can damage skin, can transmit to humans

Prevention	Treatment
Avoid contact with infected animals, often found in pet shops and kennels.	Shampoo with pyrethrin shampoo; dip with 2 percent lime sulfur dip, following package instructions; treat all exposed animals.
Keep immune system strong with good health habits; some breeds may be genetically susceptible.	Must be treated by a veterinarian with medicated shampoos and dips for several months; skin infections treated with antibiotics and healthy diet to boost immunity.
Keep ear canals clean and dry.	Treat all pets in the household; clean ears thoroughly and medicate to kill mites, as advised by your vet.
Keep dog well groomed and well cared for. Treat and keep clean all wounds/sores. Have strays with this condition treated by a vet to address larger health picture.	Remove maggots with tweezers and wash wound with povidone-iodine (Betadine) solution, followed with pyrethrin spray. Infections require veterinary treatment and oral antibiotics.
Yearly heartworm test and monthly heartworm preventive medication from one month prior to mosquito season to one month after first frost, all year in warm climates, as directed by your veterinarian.	In mild cases, treatment with a drug to kill worms; in severe cases, surgical removal of worms. Heartworm tests are required before administering heartworm preventive.
Deworming puppy as directed by veterinarian, then keeping your dog in a clean, dry environment, off dirt surfaces. Keep lawns mowed and pick up stools in environment (kennel and yard); feed healthy diet to boost immunity.	Heartworm preventive controls some intestinal worms.
Avoid drinking from streams and lakes.	Most treated with antiprotozoan medication like metronidazole (Flagyl).
Avoid contact with infected dogs.	Have a veterinarian diagnose ringworm. Treated with topical antifungal cream; bacterial infections treated with antibiotics.
Avoid contact with infected animals.	Requires treatment by a vet, including shampooing and subsequent periodic dipping with appropriate chemicals and treating dog with corticosteroids for itching and antibiotics for infected skin. Also requires spraying environment with appropriate chemicals.

on your dog:
- crusts and scales
- drainage
- hair loss
- inflammation and redness within skinfolds
- itching
- lumps
- nodules, growths
- odor
- rashes
- skin discoloration
- skin flakes
- spots
- swelling (general or localized)
- swollen hair follicles
- ulcers, non-healing wounds

INFECTIOUS DISEASES

Infectious diseases are different from inherited diseases because your dog "catches" them in some way, rather than being born with them. The best way to prevent infectious diseases is through regular vaccinations in the first year and subsequent vaccinations as recommended by your vet for your individual pet. While scientists haven't developed canine vaccines for all infectious diseases, those

Alert your veterinarian if you notice rashes, swelling, or other unusual skin conditions on your dog.

Distemper Risk

The canine distemper virus is the leading cause of death in dogs worldwide, although not in the US, where distemper vaccines are routine. All unvaccinated dogs are at high risk for distemper. Distemper is most dangerous to weak, malnourished, or immune-suppressed dogs. It attacks brain cells, skin, eyes, mucous membranes, and the gastrointestinal tract. Symptoms are a high fever of 103° to 105°F (39.5°–40.5°C), loss of appetite, lethargy, and discharge from the eyes and nose, followed by coughing, abdominal blisters, vomiting, and diarrhea. Dogs seem to recover but are then struck down again with neurological symptoms like attacks of head shaking, strange jaw movements, jerking, and seizures. Even in dogs who recover, some neurological symptoms may persist. One rare form of distemper causes hard calluses to form on paw pads. Distemper must be treated by a veterinarian. Treatment consists solely of supportive therapies like antibiotics for secondary bacterial infections, intravenous fluids for dehydration, and medications (such as anticonvulsants) to relieve symptoms. A dog's own immune system must handle the virus itself, but the best treatment is prevention through vaccination, which is almost 100 percent effective against the disease.

most serious and most common in dogs should be covered by your dog's regular vaccination protocol.

Infectious diseases often (but not always) come on suddenly and severely. They should always be diagnosed and treated by your veterinarian.

Infectious diseases come in several types:

Bacterial Diseases

Bacterial diseases are spread by contact with bacteria, typically from urine, feces, or other bodily secretions of an infected animal. In the case of Lyme disease, the bacteria are spread through a tick bite. Other examples of bacterial diseases include leptospirosis, brucellosis, bordetella, *E. coli* infections, and salmonella.

Fungal Diseases

Fungal diseases can infect the skin and mucus membranes (as with ringworm or yeast infections) or can infect a dog internally. Fungal diseases are contracted through contact with fungus spores that can enter the body through a wound in the skin or through inhalation. Fungal diseases are more common in malnourished or chronically ill dogs. They are typically characterized by diarrhea, vomiting, weight loss, and fever, and systemic forms can involve the lungs, liver, lymph nodes, brain, and spleen and can include severe neurological symptoms. Anti-fungal drugs are the typical treatment. Examples of fungal diseases include coccidioidomycosis, histoplasmosis, cryptococcosis, and blastomycosis.

Protozoan Diseases

Protozoan diseases are caused by protozoa, one-celled parasites that invade the body, typically through the ingestion of raw or undercooked meat, through contact with feces or drinking water containing the protozoa, or through feces from infected insects contaminating an insect bite. Common symptoms are severe diarrhea, lethargy, pain, discharge from the eyes and nose, and severe weight loss, depending on the protozoa. Treatment consists of an appropriate medication to kill the protozoa, such as metronidazole (Flagyl) or certain antibiotics. Examples of protozoan disease include toxoplasmosis

The most serious and most common canine diseases should be covered by your dog's regular vaccination protocol.

(more common in cats), coccidiosis, trichomoniasis, and giardiasis.

Rickettsial Diseases

Rickettsial diseases are caused by parasitic bacteria that invade cells and are usually transmitted through insects such as ticks. Examples of rickettsial diseases are canine ehrlichiosis and Rocky Mountain spotted fever.

Viral Diseases

Viral diseases are spread through contact with the bodily secretions of an infected dog, including the inhalation of airborne viruses like the canine distemper virus, bites from an infected animal (such as a bat, skunk, fox, coyote, raccoon, or, of course, another dog with rabies), or through other contact with infected urine, feces, or saliva. Other examples of viral diseases include infectious canine hepatitis, canine herpes virus, canine coronavirus, and canine parvovirus.

SYSTEM DISORDERS

Many other canine diseases affect different systems of your dog's body. While your vet should always be the one to diagnose your dog, below are some of the diseases and disorders

that can afflict different anatomical systems in your dog. Knowing what to look for can help you to help your vet.

Your dog's skin and coat may show the first symptoms of a health disorder.

Skin and Coat Problems

We've already talked about all the ways in which parasites can compromise your dog's skin and coat, but skin and coat problems exist beyond the parasitic and fungal. Your dog's skin and coat may show the very first symptoms of a health problem, so pay close attention to them, both in grooming and in your everyday interactions with your dog. Signs that your dog may have a health problem related to skin and coat include:

- bumps
- cysts
- hives
- lumps
- rashes

Disorders of the skin and coat are common in dogs. Some dogs have allergies not only to flea bites but also to foods they eat, necessitating special diets, or things they contact in their environment, from shampoos to flea collars to plants.

Allergies can manifest as hives, rashes, itchy bumps, hair loss, and hot spots. Skin can also be injured through accidents, repeated contact against a surface, or from obsessive licking. Sometimes skin conditions indicate other problems. A thyroid deficiency can cause hair loss, and so can other hormonal imbalances such as too much cortisone or too much estrogen—or even too little estrogen. Hair loss can also be caused by a number of hereditary skin diseases, but keeping your dog's coat well brushed and skin checked carefully every week will allow you to spot skin and coat problems easily.

Dogs can have allergies to flea bites, foods, plants, and other things in their environment.

Bones and Joints

Your dog, even your little toy dog, has more bones than you do! All those bones and joints can sometimes cause your dog problems. Giant breeds can grow too fast and develop bones that aren't dense enough. Many large breeds are prone to degenerative hips, and many small breeds are prone to slipping kneecaps and elbows. Long-backed breeds are susceptible to ruptured spinal disks, and any breed can develop arthritis.

Signs that your dog is suffering from a bone or joint problem include:

- apparent fatigue
- leg weakness or collapse
- limping or favoring a leg or paw
- moving more slowly than usual
- refusal or reluctance to move
- yelping after going up or down stairs, playing roughly, or jumping on or off a high surface such as a bed or couch

Hot Spot!

Hot spots are moist, pus-filled, painful patches of skin caused by a vicious cycle of itching and scratching due to allergies, dermatitis, or other skin irritations. Hot spots hurt! They are common in long-coated dogs because they can begin under mats or where skin irritation is less likely to be detected early, but hot spots can happen on any dog. Once they start, hot spots grow quickly and can be hard to resolve because dogs tend to continue to aggravate hot spots once they start. Talk to your vet about the best way to treat a hot spot, which may involve anesthetic, shaving the area, and treating with a special shampoo and an antibiotic steroid cream for several weeks, along with oral antibiotics and oral corticosteroids. Your vet may also recommend an Elizabethan collar to keep your dog from aggravating the area further.

- yelping when touched

Some of the more common musculoskeletal disorders include sprains, strains, and fractures; tendon injuries; dislocated joints; hip dysplasia (the most common cause of lameness in the back legs for dogs); Legg-Perthes disease (degeneration of the top of the leg bone, most common in toy breeds); luxating patella (slipped kneecap); elbow dysplasia (common cause of front-leg lameness, especially in large breeds); disk ruptures, especially in long-backed dogs like Dachshunds; various disorders common to rapidly growing large-breed puppies; osteoarthritis (degeneration of joints); and rheumatoid arthritis (an autoimmune disease).

Treatment for bone and joint disorders often consists of physical therapy, weight control (excess weight aggravates orthopedic problems), surgery in extreme cases, pain relief with anti-inflammatory drugs or NSAIDs (nonsteroidal anti-inflammatory drugs), and in cases of autoimmune diseases like rheumatoid arthritis, immunosuppressive drugs such as corticosteroids. Some conditions aren't curable but can be managed.

Cancer

Cancer is one of the leading causes of death in pet dogs and the leading cause of death in many breeds particularly susceptible to cancer. As pet owners have become more conscientious in caring for their

pets, dogs are living longer and cancer—usually a disease of aging in pet dogs—seems to be on the rise. Whether it is simply diagnosed more often than before is unknown, but vets are seeing and treating canine cancers more frequently.

Cancer is the rapid growth of mutant cells that replace or overwhelm healthy tissue. Not all cancers show up as lumps or growths on your dog's skin, but because so many of them do, the annual veterinary exam is essential, especially for dogs over seven years old. Internal tumors are harder to catch in their early stages, which is why physical and behavioral changes in your dog like weight loss, fatigue, lethargy, and depression are important to mention to your vet, who can then do tests that may uncover cancer.

Because dogs can develop so many different kinds of cancers, anything unusual or any changes in your dog's skin should be noted, including sores that won't heal and pigmented areas that could be melanomas or squamous cell carcinomas (skin cancers that may be caused by overexposure to the sun). Dogs can also get breast cancer, cancer of the reproductive organs (these cancers are rare in neutered dogs), bone cancer, and leukemia. Cancer is treated according to its type and in the same manner as for humans, often involving the surgical

Long-backed breeds are susceptible to ruptured spinal disks.

removal of a tumor, radiation therapy, chemotherapy, immunotherapy, or a combination of these treatments.

Cancer warning signs include:
- abdominal mass
- anemia
- blood clots beneath the skin
- bone growths
- cauliflower-like growths
- constipation
- diarrhea
- enlarged lymph nodes
- growths, lumps, or nodules beneath the skin
- internal bleeding
- mole-like pigmented areas
- red patches
- severe shortness of breath
- skin growths on the skin
- swollen limbs
- unexplained sores
- vomiting
- warts
- weight loss

More pet owners than ever before are electing to treat cancer rather than euthanize a dog with the disease, and many dogs live long, happy lives after treatment for cancer. Only you and your vet can decide how to manage cancer in your individual dog.

Circulatory System

Your dog's circulatory system is made up of his heart, veins, and capillaries. The heart pumps blood to all parts of the body, delivering nutrients and eliminating waste. When the heart doesn't work as well as it could, either through congenital abnormalities or heart disease that develops later in life, your dog can suffer from many serious and sometimes fatal conditions. Heart disease, which occurs in many breeds, ranges from minor heart murmurs to life-threatening conditions such as cardiomyopathy, the most common cause of congestive heart failure in large dogs, and congenital heart defects, such as valve malformations. The heart can also become infected by bacteria or secondarily inflamed due to other conditions like Lyme disease

Physical therapy and weight control can help with bone and joint disorders.

or distemper. Many dogs die from congestive heart failure.

Other types of circulatory problems include blood disorders like anemia and clotting disorders like von Willebrand disease (a bleeding disorder common in certain breeds) and hemophilia.

Signs your dog could have a circulatory or heart problem:
- bloated abdomen
- collapse
- coughing
- exercise intolerance
- fatigue
- lethargy
- rapid breathing
- weakness
- weight loss

At your dog's annual checkup, your vet should check your dog's heart, but remember to report any symptoms that could indicate a heart or circulation problem.

Physical and behavioral changes can help your veterinarian detect hidden cancers.

Digestive System

The digestive tract is a long passageway through your dog's body with an important job: digesting food, taking the nutrients from the food and delivering it to the body, and eliminating the excess bulk as waste. Dogs have a sturdier digestive system than humans in that they can eat some things that would make a human sick. Dogs vomit easily and readily, which can quickly eliminate food that the digestive system won't accept.

However, dogs can suffer from many disorders of the digestive system, from ulcers to motion sickness to a foreign object in the intestine to bloat (also called gastric dilation volvulus), a serious and life-threatening veterinary emergency in which the stomach fills with air and twists.

Signs your dog is having a problem with his digestive system include:
- bloating
- choking
- constipation
- coughing
- diarrhea
- dragging rear along the floor or ground during or after defecation
- excessive drooling

Pain Management Side Effects

Dogs are particularly sensitive to the kinds of medications typically used for pain relief. While certain NSAIDs may protect against cartilage damage, some like aspirin actually contribute to it. Additionally, just as in humans, NSAIDs can cause side effects like intestinal bleeding and ulcers. When it comes to pain medication, more is *not* better! Never give your dog more pain medication than prescribed. You could seriously compromise your dog's health.

But It Looks Like Cancer

Many growths and cysts on dogs are benign, such as those that often occur on the oil-producing sebaceous glands or those made of fat cells and fibrous tissue, but only a vet can tell you for sure, so point out any changes. If benign tumors interfere with a dog's movement, comfort, or even his appearance, your vet may recommend they be removed unless the risk of the surgical removal is a greater risk to your dog than the tumor itself.

- excessive thirst
- fistulas, or cysts around the rectum
- flatulence
- frequent urination
- gagging
- large appetite and weight loss together (may indicate diabetes)
- loss of appetite, accompanied by weight loss or sudden weight gain
- pain upon defecation
- polyps
- red, inflamed rectal area
- regurgitation
- restlessness or pacing
- retching without vomiting
- sensitivity to the abdominal area
- stools mixed with blood and mucus
- symmetrical hair loss coupled with a potbelly, fatigue, infertility, wasting, and weakness (could indicate Cushing's disease)

Canine Epilepsy

Epilepsy is a common nervous system disorder in many breeds that causes seizures. Grand mal seizures are short, and during these seizures, a dog will collapse and his legs will become rigid, he will lose consciousness, and then begin jerking, and in some cases, drooling. Some dogs lose bladder and bowel control. Partial seizures usually involve jerking of just one part of the body. Other causes of seizures are encephalitis, a brain tumor or abscess, stroke, kidney or liver failure, heatstroke, poisoning, head injury, or a vaccination reaction.

- unexplained weight loss or gain
- vomiting
- yellowing of skin (sign of a liver problem)

Cancer in dogs is treated according to its type and in the same manner as for humans.

Coughing, gagging, and a cough that sounds like a goose honk (a sign of a condition called "collapsing trachea," common in toy breeds) probably aren't emergencies either, unless your dog is actually choking on a foreign object. Treat constipation by making sure your dog drinks plenty of water and by adding fiber to his diet. If your dog is dragging his rear along the floor or displaying other signs that the anal sacs need emptying, have your vet or groomer empty them (or do it yourself, but have your vet show you how, and don't expect it to be a pleasant experience).

Other signs of digestive problems warrant a call to your vet as soon as possible, and any sign of bloat—retching without vomiting, restlessness and pacing, and swelling of the stomach—should be treated as an emergency. Get your dog to the vet or veterinary emergency facility immediately. Always note any non-emergency digestive changes in your grooming journal so you can mention them to your vet at your next visit.

Eyes/Ears/Nose/Throat

Your dog's eyes, ears, nose, and throat are largely visible to you, so if you pay attention during your weekly grooming exam, you may be more likely to notice when something goes wrong in these areas.

Signs that your dog is having a problem with his eyes, ears, nose, or throat include:

- bleeding from eyes, ears, nose, or mouth
- choking, coughing, gagging
- constant

> Treat constipation by making sure your dog drinks plenty of water and by adding fiber to his diet.

sneezing
- discharge from the eyes, nose, or ears
- ear scratching and shaking
- mouth breathing
- nodules or other lumps along the eyelids or nose
- redness, irritation, or swelling

Some of the more common disorders of the eyes, ears, nose, and throat include cataracts, glaucoma, progressive retinal atrophy (a degenerative eye disease leading to blindness), eyeball dislocation (most common in dogs with protruding eyes like Boston Terriers, Pugs, and Pekingese), entropion (turned-in eyelids), ectropion (rolled-out eyelid), eyelid tumors, cherry eye (a prolapsed tear gland on the third eyelid), conjunctivitis (red eye), corneal ulcers, nasal allergies, nasal tumors, collapsed nostrils (more common in flat-faced breeds), oral growths and tumors, an incorrect bite, gum disease, collapsing trachea, ear flap infections, ear mites, ear tumors, partial or total deafness, and

Eye, ear, nose, and throat disorders can cause discharge, swelling, coughing, and other symptoms.

infections of the outer, middle, and inner ear.

Keep your dog's eyes, ears, nose, and mouth in good health by keeping these areas clean and dry and by checking them often for signs of a problem.

Nervous System

Your dog's nervous system includes his brain, spinal cord, and nerves. This is information central for your dog, and damage or disease to the nervous system can result in serious neurological symptoms, like

Your Paraplegic Dog

Many dogs who become paralyzed in their rear legs due to a disk rupture or spinal accident go on to live long, happy lives with the help of wheeled carts that hold their hips up, allowing them freedom of movement. While people once commonly euthanized paralyzed dogs, today more owners are recognizing that paraplegic dogs can have a high quality of life, free of pain and full of activity. While paraplegic dogs take a little extra care, they reward their owners many times over with their joyful affection and indomitable spirit.

seizures, loss of control over bodily functions, senility, and paralysis. Dogs can suffer head and spinal injuries just like humans. The brain can become infected (encephalitis) and can develop a tumor, abscess, or arterial obstruction resulting in a stroke. Dogs can develop muscular dystrophy resulting in neurological symptoms and spinal cord degeneration (degenerative myelopathy) or sensory and motor nerve degeneration (called neuropathy). Senior dogs can even develop a condition similar to Alzheimer's disease.

Spinal cord conditions like disk ruptures, spinal tumors, spinal degeneration, spinal infection, and

> Senior dogs can develop a nervous-system condition similar to Alzheimer's disease.

spinal bone spurs can cause pain, stiffness, weakness, or partial or total paralysis (temporary or permanent). Disk ruptures indicate a veterinary emergency because without surgery, they could result in permanent paralysis, typically of the rear legs. If your dog has a long back, particular common in Dachshunds, but also in Basset Hounds, Beagles, Cocker Spaniels, Pekingese, and other long-backed dogs, and he shows any signs of a disk rupture, take him to your vet or veterinary emergency center immediately. While your vet may prescribe rest and medication instead of surgery, immediate treatment is essential for recovery.

Signs of a disk rupture include:
• depression, lethargy
• hunched position
• limping
• panting, trembling
• refusal to lower head to eat or drink
• refusal to walk up stairs or jump up onto the couch, the bed, or into a car
• sudden reluctance to climb stairs
• sudden reluctance to move
• yelping after jumping up or down
• yelping upon being patted on the head

> Spinal cord conditions can cuase pain, stiffness, or weakness.

Reproductive System

If you plan to breed your dog, you may encounter problems with the female's menstrual cycle, impotence in male dogs, reluctance to breed, false pregnancy, and any number of conditions that could result in fetal loss or malformation. Tutelage under an experienced and responsible breeder along with frequent veterinary visits can help you resolve these problems of breeding.

If you have a pet, let's hope you have already had him neutered. In Chapter 6, we mentioned that having your dog neutered greatly decreases the risk of several reproductive cancers. While neutered dogs can suffer from reproductive system disorders, such as vaginitis (a vaginal infection) or endometritis (a bacterial infection of the uterus) in females or penile infection or a strictured foreskin in males, these are relatively uncommon for healthy dogs.

Respiratory System

Your dog's respiratory system consists of his nose, mouth, throat, and trachea, which let air in and out, as well as his lungs and the muscles of his chest, which help to pump the air in and out. Obviously, respiration is essential for any living creature. Breathing supplies dogs with the oxygen they need and eliminates the carbon dioxide they don't need through exhalation, but breathing has another important function for dogs. Because dogs don't have as many sweat glands as

humans, they must pant to keep themselves cool. That's part of how dog anatomy works.

Sometimes, your dog may actually have problems with respiration. Brachycephalic (flat-faced) dogs like Bulldogs, Pugs, Pekingese, Shih Tzu, Boxers, and Boston Terriers are more likely than other breeds to suffer from respiratory problems. Because their muzzles are short, air is cooled less efficiently, so these breeds become easily overheated. These breeds also sometimes suffer from congenital deformities that hinder breathing, like collapsed nostrils and an elongated soft palate. Keep brachycephalic

> Brachycephalic (flat-faced) dogs are more likely than other breeds to suffer from respiratory problems.

dogs cool at all times and well supplied with fresh water to prevent heatstroke. A certain amount of snorting, snoring, and snuffling is natural for these breeds.

Dogs can also get laryngitis just like humans, from barking or coughing too much or due to a throat infection or tumor. Coughing is often a sign of a respiratory problem and can indicate a number of things.

Kennel cough complex is a highly contagious condition often spread around boarding kennels, the result of a number of different possible combinations of viruses and bacteria that cause coughing. A vaccinated dog will be resistant to many of the organisms that cause kennel cough complex, but any dog may contract this disease. Luckily, it isn't life-threatening, and dogs with good care and a low-stress environment usually recover quickly.

Breathing problems can signal other things, too, from a broken rib to an airway obstruction to heart failure. Always check with your vet if you notice that your dog is having trouble breathing.

Dogs with kidney failure should be monitored closely by a veterinarian and put on a special diet.

Urinary System

Your dog's urinary system consists of the kidneys, bladder, urethra, and (in males) prostate. The urinary system is a crucial system for eliminating waste from your dog's body, and when it becomes damaged or diseased, your dog will not only suffer discomfort but could suffer serious or even fatal consequences.

Signs that something is wrong with your dog's urinary system include:
- blood, mucus, or clots in urine
- drinking more often
- excessive or insufficient urination
- painful urination
- red, inflamed, or swollen penis or vulva
- sudden inability to hold urine, sudden housetraining lapses

Kidney failure is a serious disease and can result in significant damage to the kidney. Dogs with kidney failure must be monitored closely by a vet and must be on a diet that restricts salt, protein, and phosphorous.

Signs of kidney failure include:
- ammonia-like breath odor
- brownish tongue
- depression
- dry hair coat
- fatigue
- large urine output and excessive thirst
- loss of appetite
- weight loss

Dogs can get kidney stones, bladder stones, and urinary tract and bladder infections, just like humans. They can also suffer from

Pet Massage

A growing area of holistic health care for pets is pet massage. Practitioners of pet massage say it relaxes pets, helps them bond to humans, and can relieve muscle tension, pain, hypersensitivity, and even emotional conditions such as fear and anxiety. If the idea of pet massage interests you, ask your vet if she has heard of any pet massage practitioners in your area. Or massage your dog yourself by gently kneading his skin, starting at the head and face and working down the back, around the ribs, and down each leg. A pet massage is a great way to begin a weekly grooming session because it can also help you to identify any changes in your dog's skin, coat, and body.

an enlarged or infected prostate and kidney failure.

HOLISTIC HEALTH CARE FOR DOGS

As more people become interested in holistic health care for themselves, from herbal remedies and homeopathy to chiropractic care, acupuncture, and the natural foods movement, more and more pet owners are trying these therapies on their pets. The American Holistic Veterinary Medical Association (ahvma.org) has hundreds of member vets.

Holistic medicine approaches health care by looking at the big

picture, including a patient's lifestyle, diet, health habits, hygiene, genetics, psychological state, relationships, and environment. Rather than focusing only on symptoms, holistic medicine treats the whole dog, person, or cat, or whoever the patient may be. Holistic health practitioners argue that treating symptoms only masks an underlying imbalance, and that this imbalance, not its symptoms, must be addressed for healing to occur. Imbalances are typically treated with the least invasive and least harmful method possible.

Holistic health care and conventional medicine were once two different worlds, but as more people learn about what is best for their pets, more vets are embracing a complementary method, using the best of both worlds according to appropriateness. Acute situations such as broken limbs, trauma, severe infections, or emergency conditions like bloat are usually best treated with conventional medicine, but many people believe that chronic conditions like allergies, arthritis, hip dysplasia, and even certain cancers can be effectively treated using holistic methods.

Holistic health practices make sense for many pet owners because they focus on balance and prevention. When a dog gets sound nutrition, daily exercise, plenty of

Many people believe that chronic health conditions can be effectively treated using holistic methods, such as herbal therapy.

healthy human interaction, playtime, and training, that dog will be more likely to live a long, healthy life. When something does go wrong, holistic medicine seeks to balance the body to encourage self-healing.

Veterinary holistic medicine includes many different types of therapies. Some of them sound a little odd to those uninitiated into the realm of holistic health, and all have their detractors. However, thousands claim that their pets have benefited from holistic health therapies, which tend to be not only less invasive than many conventional medical treatments, but also less expensive.

The following are some of the more common techniques widely available to veterinary patients today.

Acupuncture and Acupressure

These ancient Chinese health therapies work to balance the body's energies and relieve pain by inserting needles or applying pressure, respectively, to certain key places on the

A dog who gets good nutrition, lots of human interaction, and daily exericse is more likley to live a long, healthy life.

body thought to be energy meridians. Many pet owners claim their pets have become pain-free after a course of veterinary acupuncture or acupressure treatments.

Chiropractic
Just as humans often visit chiropractors to help align, regulate, and treat musculoskeletal imbalances, veterinary chiropractors work on a dog's bones, joints, and muscles to align energy and adjust the spinal vertebrae, restoring balance and allowing the body to heal itself without impediment.

Herbal Remedies
Veterinary herbalists prescribe herbal remedies for pets as an alternative to conventional medications (although some conventional medicines are made from herbs, too). Just as with humans, please exercise caution using herbal remedies for pets. A trained veterinary herbalist can prescribe appropriate herbal remedies for your dog, but don't try to do it yourself.

Many pet owners claim their pets have become pain-free after veterinary acupuncture or acupressure treatments.

Stop and Drink the Flowers

Flower remedies are substances made from purified water and flowers designed to balance a pet's emotional energies. They are typically added to your dog's water.

Check out the Veterinary Botanical Medicine Association on the Internet (vbma.org) for more information about herbal remedies for pets.

Homeopathy

This 19th-century invention by a German medical doctor operates on the principle that "like cures like." In other words, when a substance causes certain symptoms, then very minute and diluted doses of that same substance can alleviate those symptoms. For example, if a certain herb or bacterium causes severe headaches in large amounts, then tiny diluted amounts can cure a headache. Homeopathic practitioners claim that these remedies balance the body on its deepest vibrational level so that it can heal itself. Homeopathic remedies typically contain herbs, flowers, roots, minerals, viruses, bacteria, or animal-based ingredients. They are safe because their active ingredients are so extremely diluted as to render them nontoxic, but should be used only under the direction of a homeopathic veterinarian.

A trained veterinary herbalist can prescribe appropriate herbal remedies for your dog, but don't try to do it yourself.

8

FIRST AID

I f your dog was hit by a car, in severe pain, attacked by another dog, or suffering from heatstroke, would you know what to do?

Such thoughts aren't pleasant for anyone with a family pet, and reading a chapter like this can be stressful as you consider all the things that *could* happen, even if they never do.

However, even the healthiest of dogs can encounter an accident, and knowing how to administer emergency first aid to your dog is essential for any pet owner. Better to be prepared than to be caught in an emergency without any idea what to do. Part of providing a healthy life for your pet is to be prepared in case of any emergency, even if you think the likelihood of a snakebite or poisoning or car accident seems remote for your dog. This chapter will give you general guidelines for emergency care, but always defer to your vet's advice, and don't hesitate to call your vet or emergency veterinary clinic in the case of an emergency. Use this book to help you until you can get your dog to the vet.

Knowing how to administer emergency first aid to your dog is essential for any pet owner.

YOUR CANINE FIRST-AID KIT

In an emergency, having the right supplies on hand immediately can mean the difference between life and death. Assemble a first-aid kit designed just for your dog and keep it handy so that you always know where to find it. Don't forget to bring it along when you take your dog in the car or especially on vacation.

Your first-aid kit should include the following items inside a clearly labeled container that is easily portable, such as a nylon tote bag, plastic box, or backpack:

- adhesive tape (1-inch [2.5-cm] roll)
- antibiotic ointment
- antihistamine tablets with dosage

What's the Best Medicine Again?

When it comes to emergencies, prevention is always best. Always keep your dog on a leash and supervised when out of the house, and keep trash, poisons, choking hazards, and other dangers inaccessible. In the car, keep your dog confined, and never leave him in a car, even with the windows cracked. Keep him safe from excessive cold and excessive heat, make sure he always has enough water, feed him regularly, and once again (and again and again), pay attention to your dog so that you can catch any problems before they get too serious!

instructions attached for your dog's size (ask your vet ahead of time)
- blanket or towel large enough to wrap up your dog
- card with emergency phone numbers, including:
  - ASPCA Animal Poison Control hotline: 888-426-4435
  - emergency after-hours vet clinic with address and directions
  - police or sheriff, in the case of an emergency involving another animal or person
  - your vet, including address and directions to the office in case someone else has to drive or you are panicked and forget
- compressed activated charcoal tablets with dosage instructions attached for your dog's size (ask your vet ahead of time)
- cotton balls
- digital rectal thermometer
- duct tape
- elastic (or "pressure") bandage rolls
- eyedropper
- gauze roll
- grooming clippers (to remove hair from injured areas)
- hydrocortisone ointment
- hydrogen peroxide (to induce vomiting, not for wound cleaning)
- latex or plastic gloves
- needle-nosed pliers
- nylon leash and collar
- nylon, leather, or cage muzzle, or Elizabethan collar, in case you must treat your dog when he is injured and scared
- package of gauze pads

- petroleum jelly
- rubber tubing for a tourniquet
- rubbing alcohol
- saline eye wash
- small flashlight or penlight
- small scissors for cutting tape and gauze
- surgical cleansing solution
- tweezers

HANDLING A SICK OR INJURED DOG: SAFETY FIRST!

A sick, injured, or frightened dog does not behave like a happy, contented dog and can't be handled the same way. You must take certain precautions to make sure you don't injure your friend further and that you don't get injured yourself. Follow these guidelines for proper handling to keep everyone as safe as possible.

Muzzle Safety

If your dog is injured, frightened, or in great pain, he could bite you, even if he would never consider biting under normal circumstances. That would result in two emergencies instead of one! For this reason, a muzzle is an essential item in your emergency first-aid kit.

However, misuse of a

> Assemble a first-aid kit designed just for your dog and keep it handy so that you always know where to find it.

muzzle can spell disaster. Never use a muzzle that keeps your dog's mouth shut if he is having trouble breathing or if he is vomiting, retching, choking, or unconscious. In these cases, a dog must be able to open his mouth or he could suffocate. A cage muzzle is a good option because it allows your dog to breathe through the mouth. When your dog's injuries don't involve breathing or vomiting, you can bind your dog's muzzle with a leash or a band of adhesive tape; you can also use a nylon muzzle with a Velcro closure, handy for keeping your dog from biting while tending an injury or transporting to a vet. Other options are an Elizabethan collar or a no-bite collar to keep your dog from turning his head to bite.

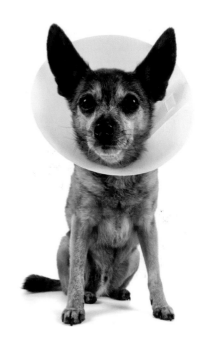

Moving and Transporting an Injured Dog

If you must move an injured dog, do so very carefully to avoid making injuries worse, especially if your dog has been hit by a car or doesn't move after jumping down from a high place, which could mean his spine is injured. Always transport a dog with a suspected spinal injury on a stretcher. Gently slide your dog to the ground so that he is lying on his side, if he isn't already, then gently slide him onto a flat surface like a piece of plywood, or even a large cutting board for a small dog.

A dog with a spinal injury should stay still, so if your dog is moving around a lot, securing a strip of duct tape over his shoulders and hips can keep him immobile.

If you must carry an injured dog in your arms, lift him correctly. Place one arm around his chest in front of his front legs and the other arm under his rump, behind the rear legs, so that all four legs are between your two arms. Move him slowly and try not to move his spine.

An Elizabethan collar will keep your dog from turning his head to bite.

EMERGENCY RESUSCITATION AND CPR

If your dog isn't breathing or if his heart has stopped, as could

happen in the case of a heart attack, electrocution, drowning, or other accident or injury, you may have to perform emergency resuscitation and/or CPR on your dog. A dog who isn't breathing has no time to travel to a vet, although you can practice these steps while en route when someone else is able to drive you and your dog.

The first step is to determine your dog's condition.

- Is your dog breathing?
- If his chest is rising and falling, and/or if you can feel breath on your cheek, check his pulse.
- If he is not breathing, pull out his tongue and check to see if anything is obstructing the airway.
- If an object obstructs the airway, see if you can hook it out with your finger.
- If you can't, perform the Heimlich maneuver on your dog. (See below.)

Safe Passage

Always move your sick or injured dog into a lying-down position on his side for transport. This position helps him to breathe more easily and is the least traumatic, especially if he is in shock or unconscious.

- If you don't see airway obstruction, check for a pulse. Does your dog have a pulse? Feel for the large femoral artery on your dog's mid thigh.
- If he has a pulse but isn't breathing, begin mouth-to-nose resuscitation (discussed later in this chapter).
- If your dog has no pulse, perform CPR (discussed later in this chapter).

The Heimlich Maneuver

If your dog is choking on something—as made evident by gagging, distress, and pawing at the throat—but still breathing, get him immediately to the vet. If his airway is obstructed and he can't breathe, open his mouth to look for a foreign object. Dogs have choked on many things, including pieces of rawhide, bone splinters, chew toys, and things they find in the trash. If you see something, try to hook it out of your dog's mouth with your finger, but be careful not to push the object farther down into your dog's throat. If you can't easily remove the item, perform the Heimlich maneuver.

> If your dog isn't breathing or if his heart has stopped, you may have to perform emergency resuscitation and/or CPR.

Here's how:

1. Put your dog on your lap with his back against your chest.
2. Put your arms around your dog's waist and make a fist.
3. Place your fist in the V at the bottom of your dog's rib cage, just above the abdominal cavity.
4. Place your other hand over your fist, then forcefully thrust your fist upward four times quickly. This should force a burst of air through your dog's throat to dislodge the object.
5. Sweep the object out with your finger.
6. If the object does not dislodge, place your mouth over your dog's nose and force air with five quick breaths into his nostrils. Some air might get past the foreign object.
7. Using the heel of your hand, strike your dog between the shoulder blades four times sharply to dislodge the object.
8. Try the finger sweep again. If the object still won't dislodge, repeat these steps until your dog is breathing.
9. When your dog is breathing again, take him immediately to the vet for follow-up care.

When your dog is breathing again, take him to the vet for follow-up care.

Emergency Breathing—Mouth-to-Nose Resuscitation

Many emergency conditions can cause your dog to stop breathing, such as choking, electrocution, heart attack, a seizure, poisoning, or shock resulting from a trauma. If your dog isn't breathing, you don't have time to get to the vet without doing something. If you aren't comfortable learning emergency breathing by reading from a book, ask your vet to demonstrate the proper technique at your next visit.

Here's what to do:

1. Check to see if your dog has a heartbeat. If not, begin CPR (see below), which includes artificial breathing.
2. Pull your dog's tongue forward with your fingers, up to the level of the canine teeth.

CPR Safety

Never practice CPR or emergency breathing on a dog who doesn't need it. You could seriously injure a dog. Even if your dog does require CPR, it could cause broken ribs and other health complications, but these are less life-threatening than the situation requiring CPR. In cases of genuine need, administering the rescue technique is worth the risk.

3. For a small dog, place your mouth over your dog's nose, forming a seal around his nostrils, and blow gently. For a large dog, also seal the lips by placing your hand around the muzzle to prevent the escape of air.

> Timely emergency care can save your dog's life.

4. Look for chest expansion. If the dog's chest doesn't expand, blow a little harder, until you see chest expansion.
5. Release your mouth after each breath, which will result in a natural exhalation and prevent overinflation of your dog's lungs.

6. Continue, administering approximately one breath every two to three seconds (three seconds for larger dogs), until your dog begins to breathe on his own, or until the heartbeat stops.

7. If heartbeat stops, begin CPR.

CPR

If your dog has no heartbeat, you must begin CPR immediately. With a larger dog, CPR is easier with two people, but you can do it alone if necessary. Here's what to do:

1. Put the dog on a flat surface on his right side. Place yourself behind the dog's back.

2. Cup your hands around a small dog's ribcage just behind the elbows. For a puppy, use the fingertips of one hand and the thumb of the other hand. For large dogs, place the heel of your hand over the widest area of the rib cage, then place your other hand on top.

3. Compress your dog's chest to about 1/4 of the chest width by pushing your hands or fingertips together in the case of a small dog,

During an emergency situation with your dog, you should *always* get to the vet as soon as possible.

or by pressing down with the heel of your hands on the ribcage of a larger dog. Compress or squeeze for 1 count, then release for 1 count, at about 100 compressions per minute for a small dog, about 80 compressions per minute for a large dog.

4. If someone is helping you, administer a breath as described above in the section on emergency breathing for every two to three compressions. If alone, administer a breath after every five compressions.

5. Continue until your dog is breathing and has a steady pulse. If your dog doesn't respond after 10 minutes, chances are slim that he will recover.

WHAT DO YOU DO IF . . .

But, you may be thinking, how do I know when to administer CPR or emergency breathing, or when to use any of those things in the first-aid kit? Many accidents can befall our pets, so consult this guide for advice on what to do when something happens. In an emergency situation, if your dog is in pain, distress, or is injured, you should *always* get to the vet as soon as possible, if you can. Fortunately, many communities have at least one 24-hour emergency veterinary clinic. Sometimes there are things you can do first, however, to help lessen the severity of the injury. Here's what to do if . . .

Your Dog Is Bleeding

If your dog has been injured and has a wound that is bleeding, the first thing to do is stop the bleeding and keep the area from becoming infected. If a wound isn't bleeding because it has clotted, leave it alone and get to a vet. However, if the wound is oozing or spurting blood, apply pressure.

Take several gauze pads from your emergency first-aid kit and place them over the wound. Press with your finger or the heel of your hand (depending on the dog's size and the wound's size) for 5 to 10 minutes. Secure the gauze with tape, adding more if necessary without removing the original gauze held against the wound. If you have bandaged the wound, watch for swelling, indicating the bandage is too tight. Loosen it but continue to apply pressure to the wound with your hand over the gauze.

If your dog is spurting blood from an artery and you can't stop the bleeding with pressure, apply a tourniquet. Only use a tourniquet if you can't control the bleeding with direct pressure. Place the tourniquet above the wound, or between the wound and the heart. Use a strip of cloth or gauze, or even a belt, and loop once or twice around the limb—again, above the wound—and insert a stick in the loop. Turn the stick to gently and slowly tighten the tourniquet. Tighten only to the point that bleeding stops. Loosen the tourniquet every 10 minutes to prevent tissue death. Loosen the tourniquet, and if blood continues to flow, let it flow for several seconds, then retighten. If bleeding has stopped, apply a pressure bandage.

Once you have the bleeding under control, transport your dog to the vet or emergency clinic, or work to stop the bleeding while someone else drives you.

When the bleeding is under control, if you can't get to a vet, you should clean the wound to prevent infection using the following procedure. If you can get to the vet, the following steps describe something similar to what your vet will do to clean and dress the wound:

1. Remove the dressing and clean the area around the wound (not the wound itself) with a surgical scrub like povidone-iodine (Betadine) or chlorhexidine-diacetate (Nolvasan) solution.
2. Rinse the wound by squirting it with tap water using a large syringe, a commercial oral irrigator, a kitchen sink or bathtub sprayer, or an outdoor hose until the wound is completely clean. A vet will probably irrigate the wound using a diluted antiseptic solution.

If your dog is bleeding and you can't get to the vet, cleaning and bandaging the wound yourself can help prevent infection.

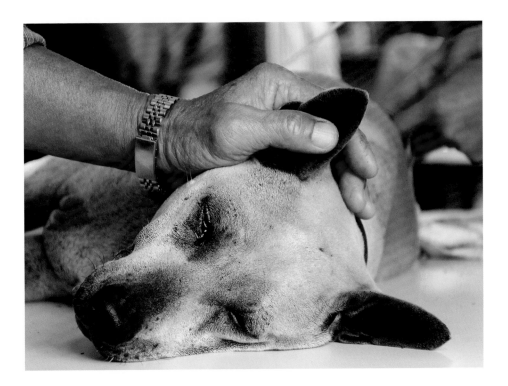

3. If cleaning the wound yourself, cover with a fresh gauze pad after cleaning and rinsing, then take your dog to the vet as soon as possible.

4. A vet will remove dying tissue and foreign matter with a forceps and scissors or scalpel, but don't try to do this yourself.

5. A vet will close an open wound with tape or sutures. Infected or oozing wounds must first be treated, which could take several days of dressing changes.

6. In the case of a puncture wound, your vet may surgically enlarge and then repair the wound.

7. Finally, the wound will probably require bandaging to keep the area clean and protected. In the absence of vet care, bandage a clean wound yourself by applying gauze over the wound in several layers, then wrapping with elastic tape tightly enough to keep the gauze in place but not so tight that it cuts off circulation. Watch for limb swelling as evidence of insufficient circulation and loosen dressing accordingly.

Dogs who have been hit by a car should be brought to a vet or emergency care clinic immediately.

8. Follow wound-care, suture, and dressing directions from your vet. In the absence of vet care, change bandages every other day and watch for drainage, swelling, or signs of infection.

Your Dog Has Been Hit by a Car

If your dog is hit by a car, he could sustain broken bones, a damaged spinal cord, wounds and bleeding, shock, even a brain injury causing coma or seizures, or he might shake himself off and walk away. No matter how bad or how mild his injuries appear, take any dog hit by a car to a vet or emergency care clinic immediately.

If your dog isn't breathing or has no heartbeat, follow the instructions above for emergency breathing or CPR. If he has bleeding wounds, follow the directions above to stop the bleeding. If your dog is in shock but breathing, transport him lying on his side to the vet via a stretcher or blanket. Keep your dog calm by talking in a soft, gentle, soothing voice and reassure him. Stay with him and keep talking. If you are panicked and upset, it will probably make your dog more panicked and upset, too, possibly aggravating his condition.

Your Dog Has Been Attacked by an Animal

Dogs are often the victims of animal attacks, usually by other dogs but also by snakes and other wild animals like raccoons, rats, badgers, possums, and coyotes. Small dogs have been killed by owls, hawks, and eagles.

If your dog has been bitten by another mammal, suspect rabies. If another dog you don't know bites your dog,

> Both dogs and humans can catch rabies when bitten by another mammal, such as a raccoon.

call the sheriff or police department immediately so that they can arrange to apprehend the dog and confirm he doesn't have rabies. If you know the owner of the dog who bit your dog, confirm that dog has a rabies vaccination (ask to see the proof), or report the incident to the authorities so they can confirm.

If a rodent, raccoon, bat, or other wild animal bites your dog, you probably won't be able to relocate the animal for testing. *Don't touch a wild animal or try to catch it yourself.* Humans can get rabies, too. Get your dog to the vet and tell him that your dog was bitten.

If a poisonous snake bites your dog, keep your dog quiet and calm to slow the spread of venom. Do not wash or touch the wound, apply ice, or make any cuts. Do not attempt to suck out the venom. These treatments don't work and could injure your dog further or even injure you. Get your dog to an emergency facility as soon as possible for treatment with antihistamines, antivenin if available, and respiratory, circulatory, and intravenous fluid support. If your dog was bitten by a poisonous snake but isn't showing signs, take him to the

Depending on the severity of the bite and the size and health of the dog, symptoms from snake venom may be nonexistent, mild, or extreme.

vet nevertheless, as some venoms don't cause symptoms immediately.

If you didn't see the attack but suspect a poisonous snake, look for the following signs:

- diarrhea
- extreme restlessness
- neurological symptoms such as sudden lack of coordination, seizures, twitching
- one or two puncture wounds
- panting and drooling
- pinpoint pupils
- severe pain
- shock
- slowed breathing
- sudden weakness
- swollen, discolored tissue
- vomiting

Depending on the severity of the bite and the size and health of the dog, symptoms may be nonexistent, mild, or extreme. Sometimes even with veterinary care, the bite will be fatal, but the sooner your dog is treated, the better his chances for recovery.

Your Dog Is Drowning

Dogs are natural swimmers, but that doesn't mean they can't drown if they fall through ice, are swept away by a current or floodwaters, or if they are unable to get out of a swimming pool or lake. Some breeds are particularly susceptible to drowning because they are not built to be in the water, such as English Bulldogs and some other Bulldog-type breeds, but drowning could happen to any dog, even a water dog like the Labrador Retriever.

Dog-on-Dog Aggression

Many dogs are naturally dog-aggressive, even those who would never think of biting a human. Small dogs are at risk for severe injury from attacks by larger dogs, and large dogs, particularly of the same sex, and in the case of males, those who are unneutered, are likely to squabble. Depending on the breed and the individual, squabbles can result in serious injuries. If all involved dogs are vaccinated for rabies, treat wounds as for any other injury.

After removing a dog from the water, immediately hold him upside down by the chest or rear legs if you can, to help excess water run out of his nose and mouth. If he is too heavy, try to lay him down on an angled surface so that his head is lower than his body. Check for breathing and heartbeat, and administer emergency breathing or CPR as indicated in those sections earlier in this chapter.

Your Dog Has Been Electrocuted

Puppies are notorious for chewing on electrical cords, but older dogs can also be electrocuted if they come into contact with a downed power line or are hit by lightning, or even if they are in the vicinity of a lightning strike.

Never touch a dog in contact with an electric cord, or you could also be electrocuted. Shut off power, pull the plug, and then check for breathing and heartbeat. If either of these is absent, administer emergency breathing or CPR as described in those sections earlier in this chapter. If your dog is conscious and breathing, take him to the vet to check for heart damage, pulmonary damage, mouth burns, or neurological damage.

You Think Your Dog Is Poisoned

A dog's world is filled with potential poisons: pest poisons, antifreeze, human medications, overdoses of pet medications, garbage, chocolate, household cleaners and chemicals, even poisonous plants in your home or garden. Any of these items could poison a dog if ingested, and of course, avoiding poisoning by keeping all poisonous substances out of reach of your dog is the best way to prevent an issue. Accidents happen, however.

In the case of poisoning, or suspected poisoning, always get your dog to a veterinarian as soon as possible. Call first to see what you should do, and so that the staff knows you are coming. Poisons can cause many different issues, and a veterinarian is the best authority for determining the kind of treatment

Dogs who are drowning should be removed from the water and checked for breathing and heartbeat.

your dog requires. While getting the poison out is often important, the process of poison leaving the body can sometimes cause even more harm, so this is a job best left to the professionals. If you know or suspect what poisoned your pet, bring the medication container, packaging, or any other information with you.

You could also call the Pet Poison Helpline at 800-213-6680 or the ASPCA Animal Poison Control hotline at 888-426-4435. Post these numbers so they are always available, just in case. This puts an expert on the other end of the line who can advise you on what you might be able to do at home. There will probably be a fee associated with the call, but it will likely be minimal.

Call your vet, the Pet Poison Helpline (800-213-6680), or the ASPCA Animal Poison Control hotline (888-426-4435) for instructions if your dog has ingested poison.

Your Dog Has Heatstroke and/or Dehydration

A dog exposed to high heat can experience a dangerous rise in body temperature. Dogs don't handle heat as well as humans, particularly dogs with short, flat faces and with long heavy coats with origins in arctic climates. Dogs often suffer heatstroke when they are left inside cars in warm weather because the temperature inside a car can rise quickly compared to the temperature outside, particularly on a sunny day. Dogs also may experience heatstroke

Dangerous Indoor & Outdoor Plants

Some of the more common indoor plants that are poisonous include the following (this is a partial list—many other houseplants can cause poisoning):

- amaryllis
- asparagus fern
- azalea
- bird-of-paradise
- Boston ivy
- caladium
- chrysanthemum (mums)
- creeping Charlie
- crown of thorns
- dieffenbachia (dumbcane)
- elephant's ear
- ivy (many types)
- mother-in-law plant
- nightshade
- philodendron
- poinsettia
- tuberous begonia
- umbrella plant

Many different outdoor plants can cause poisoning, from mild to severe. Ask your vet what plants in your area are toxic, since outdoor plants vary widely according to geographical location. Some of the more common and ubiquitous outdoor plants that can cause poisoning in your dog include the following (this is a partial list—many other plants can cause poisoning):

- almond tree
- apricots
- azalea
- castor bean
- cherry tree
- daffodil
- delphinium
- English holly
- foxglove
- jimsonweed
- lupine
- mayapple
- mock orange
- morning glory
- mushrooms
- peach tree
- periwinkle
- poppies
- potatoes
- rhododendron
- rhubarb
- spinach
- tomato vines
- wild cherry
- wisteria

if they exercise too much when the weather is hot and humid, or if they are muzzled while under a dryer at the groomer's. Dogs confined in small warm areas without proper ventilation, on hot surfaces like concrete, or who suffer from a fever due to illness may also suffer from heatstroke.

Signs of heatstroke include heavy panting, labored breathing, a bright red tongue and mouth, thick saliva, and vomiting. Rectal temperature can rise to 104° to 110°F (40°–43.5°C). The dog may have bloody diarrhea, go into shock, or suffer collapse, seizure, coma, and death.

Dogs suffering from heatstroke must be cooled quickly. Bring the dog into a cool place such as an air-conditioned building or at least in the shade on a cool surface. Spray him with a hose (make sure the water is cool, not hot, if the hose has been in the sun), or immerse him in a tub of cool water. Put a wet dog in front of a fan and monitor rectal temperature every 10 minutes until it reaches 103°F (39.5°C).

If you have a dog who likes chewing, deny access to potentially poisonous plants.

At this point, dry the dog and stop cooling him to prevent hypothermia or shock.

Sometimes a dog with heatstroke is also dehydrated, but dogs can also become dehydrated after an episode of vomiting and/or diarrhea. Dehydration can cause subsequent heatstroke.

Signs of dehydration include loss of skin elasticity, dry mouth, dry gums, thick saliva, sunken eyes, collapse, and shock. If you think your dog is dehydrated, take him to the vet or emergency vet clinic immediately for intravenous fluid replacement.

If your dog is only mildly dehydrated and isn't vomiting, use a squirt bottle or syringe to give him an electrolyte solution made for children. Give your dog about 2 to 4 milliliters per pound (0.5 kg) of body weight every hour.

To prevent heatstroke, keep your dog cool during the hot summer months.

Heatstroke Prevention

Prevent heatstroke by never leaving your dog in a car, even when you don't think it's very hot (especially when the sun is out). Also, don't let your dog spend too much time in hot humid weather, restrict exercise in severe heat, and make sure that he always has plenty of cool, fresh water.

Your Dog Has Hypothermia or Frostbite

A dog left outside in cold weather for too long can suffer from hypothermia, a dangerous drop in body temperature. Dogs with short coats, very young or very old dogs, and dogs who get wet in the cold are particularly susceptible to hypothermia.

Suspect hypothermia if your dog is shivering, listless, and lethargic, has a weak pulse, and has a temperature lower than 95°F (35°C). Hypothermic dogs may be revived after longer periods without heartbeat or breathing. A hypothermic dog must be gradually warmed. Wrap him in a blanket and take him inside a warm place. Dry him well with towels if he is wet. Encourage the dog to drink water with sugar or honey dissolved in it. If your dog's temperature is below 95°F (35°C), call your vet for instructions and apply warm water bottles wrapped in towels to your dog's chest. Continue until rectal temperature reaches 100°F (37.8°C).

Suspect frostbite, particularly common on tails, tips of ears, pads of feet, and the scrotum, if skin in these areas is very pale or blue and becomes swollen and red upon warming, then sometimes black. Frostbitten tissue dies and will peel or fall away within a few weeks. Apply warm water to frostbitten tissue until color returns. Do not use hot water or hot air, and never rub frostbitten tissue, as this causes tissue damage. Frostbite can be very painful. Restrain a dog who becomes upset or tries to irritate a frostbitten area, and see your vet for further treatment.

Your Dog Has Been Burned

Dogs can be burned in many ways: by electrocution, the sun, a hot surface, a hot liquid, or

> Suspect hypothermia if your dog is shivering, listless, and lethargic, has a weak pulse, and has a temperature lower than 95°F (35°C).

corrosive chemicals. If your dog is burned, see a vet immediately. Burns require professional attention to protect skin, and large burns may induce shock and require secondary treatment for infection and fluid loss.

For a small, superficial burn, apply a cool cloth (not ice) to the area for 20 minutes to minimize injury and for pain relief. Clip hair from the burn, wash skin gently with an antiseptic solution, and apply antibiotic ointment. Bandage carefully and change the dressing daily, reapplying antibiotic ointment with every dressing change.

Chemical burns should be flushed with water for 10 minutes before dressing and blotted dry, and should be checked by a vet. Wear gloves when treating chemical burns to

prevent getting burned yourself.

> Dogs who have suffered falls or heavy impacts should be checked for fractures.

Your Dog Has a Broken Limb

If your dog is hit by a car or jumps or falls from a great height, or if you have a toy breed puppy who jumps out of someone's arms or is accidentally stepped on, suspect a broken bone. Signs of a bone fracture include a misshaped limb, swelling, redness, pain, lameness, or in the case of a compound fracture, bone protruding through skin. Fractures can result in dangerous blood loss, damage to internal organs, and shock. Dogs in extreme pain may be likely to bite, so use a muzzle if necessary.

Warm Your Dog Safely

If your dog has hypothermia, do not treat him by dunking him into a hot bath or warming him with a blow-dryer, as these could cause tissue damage. Instead, warm your dog gradually with warm compresses and gentle handling.

Clean any open wounds and splint bones in their broken position for transport to your vet. Do not attempt to straighten a broken bone before splinting. Leave this to your vet. Splinting or securing broken limbs is done to prevent further damage in transport, not for the purpose of healing the fracture.

Splint lower-limb fractures using a folded newspaper or thick piece of cardboard secured to the limb with gauze or tape. Upper-limb, spinal, head, or torso fractures are best handled by immobilizing the dog during transport, such as by duct tape and a stretcher as described earlier in this chapter, or by keeping the dog calm and still.

Your Dog Is in Shock

Shock is a condition caused by trauma in which the body's circulatory and respiratory systems slow drastically, causing a lack of sufficient oxygen and blood flow to the body. This is an emergency condition requiring immediate medical attention. Suspect your dog is going into shock if he has suffered a trauma, such as a heart attack, severe accident, allergic reaction, or poisoning, and begins to pant, suffer an increased heart rate, and has a bright red mouth and tongue. Advanced shock is evident from pale skin and gums; cold extremities; lowered body temperature, heart rate, pulse, and respiration rate; lethargy; and loss of consciousness or coma.

If your dog isn't breathing or has no heart rate, administer emergency breathing or CPR, as described earlier in this chapter. Control bleeding of any wounds, and if

Monitor your dog closely if he has an increased heart rate and seems to be panting excessively.

possible, splint or stabilize broken bones as described earlier in the chapter. Rest your dog on his right side, and using a stretcher or blanket, take him immediately to a vet or emergency vet clinic.

During the course of treatment and transport, stay calm and talk in a gentle soothing manner to your dog. Even if he doesn't appear to be conscious, he may be affected by your behavior. Fear and anxiety could worsen his condition.

Your Dog Has an Eye Injury

If your dog's eye is injured or if he loses an eye (this sometimes happens in breeds with protruding eyes like Pekingese, Pugs, Maltese, and Boston Terriers), you must act quickly. A traumatized dog can sometimes strain so hard that his eye bulges out to the point that it becomes dislocated. Swelling in the eye socket makes relocation of the eyeball difficult, so time is of the essence. Get to the closest emergency facility right away. Carry the dog, eye covered with a wet cloth, and keep the dog from bothering the eye socket.

Your Dog Is in Pain and You Don't Know Why

Sometimes you know your dog is in distress but you have no idea why, because you didn't see what happened or because there is no obvious explanation. When your dog is in pain, call your vet and describe the symptoms or take him to an

Anaphylactic Shock

Shock is caused by trauma, but anaphylactic shock is a specific allergic reaction to such things as penicillin, insect venom, or a vaccination. Signs of anaphylactic shock include a skin reaction at the sting or vaccination site, as well as general signs of shock such as diarrhea, vomiting, labored breathing, a swollen throat, weakness, severe restlessness, collapse, and coma. Without treatment, dogs can quickly die from anaphylactic shock, so transport your dog to a vet immediately.

emergency clinic. Remember to stay calm, be soothing, and reassure him that you are there to take care of him.

It's frustrating to have a suffering pet and not know the reason why, but the way you respond to emergency situations will often directly impact how your dog responds. Be the responsible caretaker and stay calm, act quickly and rationally, and do everything you can to ease your pet's anxiety and pain.

SENIOR HEALTH AND WELLNESS

9

After the challenges of puppyhood and the happy equilibrium of adulthood, dogs, like people, enter those golden years. Maybe you've had some health issues along the way, or maybe not, but here you are—your dog has made it to ripe old age. Congratulations!

The average age for reevaluating your dog's care and granting him senior status is seven years, but dogs vary in their expected life span almost as much as they vary in size. The smaller the dog, the longer he is likely to live. While a Great Dane is heading into senior status at age five or six, a Chihuahua is just barely ending his adolescence. Large and giant breeds like Newfoundlands, Bloodhounds, Irish Wolfhounds, and Mastiffs are lucky to make it to age 11 or 12, but toy breeds often make it to 17, 18, and sometimes even 19 or 20 years old. Experts say the maximum canine life span is probably about 27 years, but a 27-year-old dog would be exceedingly rare.

However, in many ways, as they say, age is just a number. More important than your dog's age is his physical status. Just because your dog is getting old doesn't mean you must suddenly cut his calories,

Entering the senior years requires heightened vigilance about changes in your dog's body and behavior.

change his food, or force him to "take it easy." (Your grandma doesn't like that either!) But entering the senior stage of life does necessitate a heightened vigilance about changes in your dog's body and behavior. Diseases like cancer, heart disease, and diabetes, along with many other conditions, become more common with age in both dogs and people, so paying closer attention and increasing those annual vet visits to once every six months can ensure that your dog lives as long as possible.

THE SIGNS OF CANINE AGING

When your dog gets older, his body doesn't work quite as well as it once did. He may not see, hear, smell, or taste as well. When your dog can't see or hear as sharply as before, he may become more irritable or nervous because he isn't always immediately aware of what is going on around him. A touch from behind could startle him. Strangers might seem more threatening if he hasn't detected their approach. He may become more likely to guard his food.

Your dog may also lose control over some of his functions. He may begin to have occasional housetraining accidents, lose control of his back legs, suffer respiratory problems and fatigue that could indicate heart disease (or other diseases), or his digestive system may become more sensitive. He may even get disoriented or suffer other signs of senility.

Depending on the dog, the breed, the size, and the age, functional decline can begin anywhere from 5 years to 15 years. Depending on what happens to your dog, you can make changes in his lifestyle and care to head off serious health problems and to make him feel more comfortable and secure. If your older dog starts

Make your dog feel as comfortable as possible as he enters his senior years.

showing age-related changes, talk to your vet about increasing annual exams to twice a year and make a note to let your vet know about the changes you've noticed so that she can do the appropriate examinations and tests. Many of these symptoms of age-related decline or disease are the same as symptoms to watch for in younger dogs developing a disease, but they become more likely to occur as a dog ages.

Remember that some signs of aging are inevitable as a dog's body ages, such as slight decreases in activity, less energy, and decreased sharpness of vision and hearing. Conditions like age-related deafness may be incurable, but many symptoms signify diseases and other conditions that can be treated and are not inevitable with age. Seek veterinary advice and care for any of the following:

- bloody or pus-filled discharge from any orifice
- changes in bowel habits including diarrhea or constipation
- cloudy eyes or other signs of vision loss
- coughing
- disorientation, failure to recognize familiar people, seeming to get lost in the house
- increased pulse
- increased temperature

Seek veterinary advice and care for symptoms such as breathing trouble, disorientation, and bodily growths.

- increase in thirst and frequency of urination
- loss of appetite
- lumps, nodules, or growths anywhere on the body
- rapid breathing or difficulty breathing
- sudden exercise intolerance
- swollen gums and/or lost teeth
- unusual fatigue
- weakness
- weight loss
- wheezing or panting

PREVENTIVE GERIATRIC CARE

The most important thing you can do to ensure that your dog's senior years are healthy is to practice good health care throughout his puppyhood and adult years. A healthy young dog is more likely to be a healthy old dog.

Once your dog is a senior, however, you can make certain changes in his routine and care to help keep him as healthy and comfortable as possible.

Aging Skin and Coat

As a dog ages, his skin becomes less supple and his coat becomes drier. He is also more likely to develop tumors, nodules, cysts, and sores on his aging skin. Increase your weekly grooming exam to every other day or even daily for your senior dog, rather than every week. Not only will your dog enjoy the added attention and handling from you, but you will be more likely to find skin changes that you can show your vet. If a bump turns out to be an infection or even a cancer, you'll find it early and increase the chances of effective treatment.

More frequent brushing will also help to keep your dog's coat healthier by distributing oils. A moisturizing coat conditioner or spray can help to keep the coat shiny, too. Just because your dog is old doesn't mean that he can't look and feel good.

Just because your dog has aged doesn't mean that he can't look and feel good.

Weight Management

Because older dogs tend to be achier and less interested in exercise, they also tend to require fewer calories. However, pampering owners may be inclined to feed their aging dogs even more food, just because they think their older dogs need to have something to enjoy. Nothing could be more dangerous for your aging pet! Obesity is not only the most common nutrition-related disease of adult dogs but also one of the most common health conditions of older dogs. Obesity aggravates many other conditions of aging, like arthritis, heart disease, and diabetes. Your achy pet will be even achier if he is carrying around extra weight. Joints will deteriorate faster, muscles will grow weaker, the heart will have to work harder, exercise will become more uncomfortable, and your dog will decline more quickly. Overweight dogs are more likely to succumb to the diseases of aging faster and they may indeed live shorter lives.

Feed your dog according to his activity level. Some seniors stay very active to the end of their lives, but those who slow down don't need as much food. If you notice that your dog's shape is changing, that nice waist tuck is disappearing, those ribs

> **Keeping your senior dog at a healthy weight eases various health conditions.**

are becoming impossible to find, then decrease your dog's food intake. Cutting down on treats may be all that is required.

If your dog seems to be gaining weight inexplicably, talk to your vet, because this could indicate a medical problem. Stomach bloating could also be due to a tumor.

The bottom line is that the two most important keys to keeping your senior dog (or anyone) at a healthy weight are to make sure he gets daily moderate exercise and a healthy diet with an appropriate number of calories. Your senior dog needs approximately 30 calories per pound (0.5 kg) of body weight, more (35 to 40) if he is very active, and a little less (25) if he is very sedentary. Check your dog food label for calorie content or estimate that dry kibble has about 1,600 calories per pound (0.5 kg), canned about 500 calories per pound (0.5 kg). Then, adjust according to whether your dog does well on the diet. Hunger is not an indication that he isn't getting enough calories. Instead, monitor his appearance and energy level. If you are unsure about how much to feed your senior dog, check with your vet for a personalized recommendation.

Arthritis and Aging Muscles

As bones, joints, and muscles age, they experience wear and tear. Joints become stiffer and more painful, and muscles become weaker and less flexible. You may have heard that exercise and weight lifting are important for aging humans to fight the age-related decline of muscles, bones, and joints. Older dogs also benefit immensely from regular exercise, which helps keep muscles toned and joints freer. Pay attention to how your dog tolerates exercise, however. Don't push him to the point of pain. Your vet can prescribe medication for a dog with arthritis, but exercise is equally important.

Senior Kibble?

Your dog is seven. Should you switch to that food in the pet store labeled "Senior Formula"? Not necessarily. If your dog is still active and doing well on his food, you have no reason to switch formulas. If your dog is less active than he once was, you should decrease the number of calories he consumes each day but not necessarily change the type of food. Senior formulas typically have fewer calories and more fiber, which can add bulk to your dog's diet and help him feel less hungry on fewer calories. But look at the protein content. Senior formulas with reduced protein aren't a good idea for aging dogs who may need more protein to fight muscle atrophy. The one exception: Dogs with kidney or liver disease do need low-protein diets, as prescribed by a vet.

Hip dysplasia also occurs with greater frequency in older dogs, especially in larger breeds. Large dogs fed too many calories as puppies are even more prone to the disease, and if your dog experiences weakness, pain, or loss of function in his legs or hips, ask your vet about the possibility of dysplasia. A dog with mild dysplasia may not require any treatment, but more serious cases typically require pain relief in the form of NSAID analgesics, medication to relieve joint inflammation and repair cartilage, restriction of certain activities like running and jumping (while still maintaining an exercise regimen including nonstressful activities like swimming and walking), and in extreme cases, surgery, ranging from simple repositioning of hips or removal of certain muscles to a total hip replacement.

Regular gentle exercise keeps your senior dog's muscles toned and joints healthy.

Long in the Tooth, Sore in the Gums

Good dental care throughout life is important for keeping teeth and gums healthy in older dogs, but even so, older dogs may need their teeth cleaned more often than younger dogs. If you've never had your dog's teeth professionally scaled by a vet, this procedure may become necessary later in life. Some individual dogs require cleaning more than others, as they seem to accumulate more tartar. Gums in older dogs may become infected, which can lead to pain, tooth loss, and difficulty eating. This can debilitate an old dog quickly. Oral bacteria and infection can travel to the heart, so good dental hygiene is more than a matter of aesthetics.

Check your senior dog's teeth every day and keep them well brushed, especially if your dog can no longer chew on hard biscuits. Have your vet look over teeth and gums closely and scale them if necessary at least twice a year. This should be part of the regular checkup, but remember to mention any oral changes or signs that your dog is experiencing dental or periodontal pain.

Cognitive Dysfunction Syndrome

When your dog ages, his brain ages, too, in a variety of ways. Plaque deposited in the brain can cause cell death and brain shrinkage. Aging brains have lower oxygen levels and experience changes in certain neurotransmitters like serotonin, norepinephrine, and dopamine. The result is a decline in brain function manifesting as senility. This disease is similar to Alzheimer's disease in humans, and about half of senior dogs over age 10 will probably exhibit some symptoms to varying degrees.

Recently, veterinary medicine has discovered ways to improve the

symptoms of cognitive dysfunction syndrome through medication. See your vet if your dog experiences any of the following signs of age-related neurological decline:

- changes in sleep habits
- disorientation

Genetic Test Certification

The Orthopedic Foundation for Animals (OFA) keeps records of genetic tests done on purebred dogs so that breeders can register their dogs as certified free of hip dysplasia, elbow dysplasia, autoimmune thyroiditis, congenital cardiac disease, or patellar luxation. OFA also tracks abnormalities based on DNA testing that indicate other conditions specific to certain breeds, like progressive retinal atrophy and von Willebrand disease. A breeder should be able to show you proof that the parents of a litter of puppies have been certified free of hip dysplasia and other diseases or conditions to which a particular breed may be prone. However, parents certified free of hip dysplasia or other inherited conditions does not guarantee that your dog won't develop those conditions later in life. For more information on certification against certain inherited diseases, visit OFA's website at offa.org.

- failure to recognize familiar people or respond to familiar verbal cues
- getting lost or "stuck" in familiar areas like the house or yard
- housetraining accidents that can't be attributed to other health problems
- increasing failure to greet people when they come home (could also be a sign of hearing loss)
- showing little or no interest in activities once enjoyed, like petting, playing, chasing, or retrieving (could also be related to arthritis or other movement-induced pain)
- showing little or no interest in family members
- strange behaviors like circling, shaking, weakness, or aimless wandering

Testing for Better Health

See your vet if your dog experiences signs of age-related neurological decline.

As recommended above, senior dogs can be better assured of proper care if they have a physical exam by a vet twice a year instead of just once a year. During the physical exam for a senior dog, your vet may decide that certain tests are required, based on symptoms that you've mentioned or changes that she notices. While more tests cost more money, they are also an invaluable tool for catching diseases in the early stages, and they could significantly extend your dog's life span and life quality if they give your vet the information she needs to treat a developing health problem.

During a checkup for a senior dog, your vet should give your dog a thorough physical exam to look for skin changes, lumps and bumps, and any infections, parasites, or painful areas. She will also do a complete blood workup and a urinalysis. Your vet should check your dog's teeth and clean and scale them if necessary. (You may need to schedule a separate appointment for this procedure.) Also, if your dog is experiencing certain symptoms of liver, kidney, or heart disease, your vet may decide to do liver and kidney function tests, a chest X-ray, or an electrocardiogram.

YOUR SENIOR DOG'S SPECIAL NEEDS

Your senior dog has a few other special needs beyond scheduling more frequent vet checkups and grooming. As your dog ages, his senses dull, his body doesn't work as well, and he may become more irritable, more confused, and more in need of comfort, assistance, and reassurance. It isn't easy getting old, and your dog may become startled more easily, behave more irritably, or be reluctant to do the things he used to do because he is achy and sore or because he doesn't understand why he can't move the way he used to move. Try to protect him from situations that will put him under extra stress if he isn't feeling well, such as subjecting him to lots of chaos, small children who want to poke and prod, or unnecessary time away from you.

To make your dog feel more comfortable and safer in his old age, make an effort to spend a little more quiet time together. Take him on a daily walk, but don't push the pace beyond what he can handle. Be patient with your dog and let him have his space when he needs it.

If your dog has a hard time getting around due to hip dysplasia, disk disease, or arthritis, make things easier. A carpet-covered board can

Safety for Senile Dogs

A dog suffering from cognitive dysfunction syndrome (which is similar to Alzheimer's disease in humans) could easily become lost if he wanders out of the house or yard. While all dogs should be kept safely confined, senile dogs require particular vigilance because they may not be able to find their way back. This is of particular concern for dogs who always stick close to home and whose owners have never had to worry about keeping them on a leash or within a fence, because they may be less accustomed to being careful to keep their pets confined. Remember, a senile dog may want to come home but may be unable to, even if he is only a short distance away. Keep your aging pet safe.

serve as a ramp up to your small dog's favorite chair or the bed, if your dog sleeps with you. Rearrange food and water bowls to minimize trips up and down the stairs.

As throughout your dog's youth and adulthood, vigilance is the best way to determine what your dog really needs. Just because your dog is aging doesn't mean he can't continue to exercise vigorously. If your dog has been healthy and exercised regularly throughout life, he may not slow down much at all. Only by paying attention to your dog's behavior and physical symptoms can you best monitor what he can and can't do and how much extra help he needs.

Some dogs can be revitalized by the introduction of a new puppy into the home, and other dogs may react against an overzealous intruder. Only you can judge if your dog would enjoy the company of a younger dog or if a puppy's constant quest for play would be more irritating than stimulating for your senior. If you do introduce a new puppy to the home, don't forget to give your senior dog the seniority he deserves, along with plenty of attention, love, and reassurance so that he doesn't feel he is being replaced but instead feels he is gaining a nonthreatening buddy.

No matter how good or bad your senior dog is feeling, don't forget

Consider household accommodations for senior dogs who have trouble getting around.

to continue spending quality time together so that your dog knows he is loved and is able to enjoy his final years in your close company. That's what he really wants.

SAYING GOODBYE

The hardest part of loving a dog must surely be when you have to say goodbye. Whether your dog succumbs to old age on his own or whether you make the decision to put an end to his pain and suffering when his quality of life is no longer tolerable, saying goodbye to a pet is a heart-wrenching experience.

If your aging pet is suffering pain that can't be remedied and if he has declined to the point that he no longer enjoys life, you may feel it is your responsibility as his guardian to put an end to his suffering. The decision to euthanize your pet is a difficult one— one of the most difficult decisions you may ever make. But if you grant your pet the ultimate kindness of ending his suffering, don't feel guilty. You have done the right thing.

Don't Redecorate

If your dog is losing his sight, make an effort to keep furniture in the same place. This isn't the time to redecorate the living room. Your vision-impaired dog is familiar with a certain layout to the house, and moving things around can confuse and scare him.

And if you aren't sure? If your pet is debilitated but can still enjoy his life, then you may decide to let nature take its course. Talk to your vet, who may be able to give you advice. Your vet can determine, when you may not be able to, how much pain your dog is feeling, and can also help you to understand your dog's prospects for recovery and pain relief.

Whatever you and your vet decide, losing a beloved pet isn't easy. People often take many days, months, even years to stop feeling sad. You may become depressed or cry a lot. It's completely natural. Many books and websites are devoted to counseling and supporting those who have lost a pet. Gone are the days when those grieving over the loss of a pet feel silly for their sadness. Pets have become valued family members, and so many have lost pets that people understand. Seek support for your grief.

In the end, though dogs may not live as long as humans, the relationships we form with them and the love and affection we share make the dog–human relationship something beautiful and special. If you have done your part to give your dog a happy life with good health care, training, and lots of time together, you have given your dog the best possible life he could have. He has enriched your life, too. People all over the world who have loved and lost their pets agree: Loving and caring for a dog is worth every moment.

GLOSSARY OF DISORDERS AND DISEASES

Addison's disease: Also called hypoaldosteronemia or hypoadrenocorticism, this is a condition caused by adrenal dysfunction and failure to produce sufficient corticosteroids, characterized by low sodium but high potassium levels in the blood. This life-threatening disease is very difficult to diagnose, but once identified, it can be controlled effectively with medication. See *Cushing's syndrome*, *hyperkalemia*.

allergies: Hypersensitivities to certain environmental agents, or "allergens." The first level of autoimmune hypersensitivity. Symptoms in dogs are usually dermatological (skin rash), but respiratory symptoms like human hay fever may sometimes occur. See *hives*.

amyloidosis: The deposition of amyloid proteins in body tissues, especially of concern in the kidneys. See *Shar-Pei Fever*, *kidney failure*.

anal atresia: A rare congenital condition in which a membrane separates the rectum from the anus. In severe cases there may be no anus. Surgery is the only possible treatment. The full Latin name of this condition is *atresia ani*.

anesthesia sensitivity: Unusual reaction to anesthetics, sometimes resulting in death. Although there is much anecdotal evidence of different probabilities of anesthesia sensitivity among breeds, there is no reliable evidence. In any case, there is a great deal of individual variation even within a breed.

anterior cruciate ligament injury: A rupture or tear of a major ligament in the knee, causing pain and lameness. Obese dogs are more at risk. Early diagnosis improves the prognosis. Surgical repair requires extensive postoperative care and therapy.

aortic stenosis: A thickening or narrowing on or near the aortic valve, reducing blood flow through the valve. When the stenosis is just below the valve, it is called *subaortic stenosis* (q.v.).

arthritis: Inflammation of joints related to degeneration of cartilage. Can be caused by injury; infection; or an *autoimmune* response (q.v.). Treatment depends on the cause and can include surgery and medication.

aseptic meningitis: Also called sterile meningitis, a condition in which the linings of the brain (meninges) are inflamed but no bacterial infection is present. There may be mycobacterial or viral infection, and it can occur without a pathogen, as a result of drug treatment or an autoimmune condition.

autoimmune disease: A condition in which the body's immune system targets one or more of its own tissues. The severity of the disease depends in part on which tissues or organs are attacked by the immune system. Many canine autoimmune diseases are similar to those known in humans, such as rheumatoid arthritis; *degenerative myelopathy* (q.v.); and autoimmune hypothyroidism. See *autoimmune thyroiditis*, *immunoproliferative small intestinal disease (IPSID)*, *myasthenia gravis (MG)*.

autoimmune hemolytic anemia (AIHA): Also known as *immune-mediated hemolytic anemia (IMHA)*. The destruction of red blood cells by the body's immune system, resulting in anemia (decreased red blood cell count). Symptoms may appear suddenly or gradually. Diagnosis is through lab tests, and treatment typically uses corticosteroids or stronger immunosuppressant drugs.

autoimmune thyroiditis: The destruction of the thyroid by the body's immune system, leading to hypothyroidism (low levels of thyroid hormones). There is a clearly established genetic component to this disease, and it is more prevalent in certain breeds than in others. Because of the importance of the thyroid in so many bodily functions, symptoms of this condition are extremely variable, and it can affect most of the body's systems, as well as the dog's behavior and personality. Various lab tests can confirm a diagnosis, and screening of all breeding stock will work to lower the incidence of this problem.

back problems: Dogs can suffer from a variety of back problems, ranging from a pulled muscle to a herniated disk. Causes include trauma during work or exercise; injury from accidents; and genetic or developmental malformations. Symptoms range from pain to paralysis. Treatment depends on the cause and may include medication; surgery; therapy; and enforced rest.

Beagle Pain Syndrome (BPS): A type of sterile encephalitis/arteritis also known as necrotizing vasculitis. While other breeds may be affected, it is very common in Beagles. Symptoms include neck pain and spasms or stiffness of the neck and front legs, and they are very similar to those of other serious conditions like meningitis or cervical disk damage, which require very different treatment. Thus, correct diagnosis is crucial. Treatment usually involves anti-inflammatory steroids, sometimes in massive doses. Although more common in older dogs, very young dogs can be stricken. There is no cure, but lifelong treatment is often effective.

bladder stones: Urinary stones found in the bladder. See *cystinuria*, *urolithiasis*.

bloat: Technically gastric torsion or gastric dilatation-volvulus (GDV), this life-threatening condition manifests very quickly, often after eating. Although the common name of the affliction refers to the distention that often occurs, there is not always a visible swelling of the abdomen. Gas and/or fluid is trapped in the stomach, sometimes because of torsion or twisting, and the dog can die in a very short time. Immediate veterinary intervention is the dog's only hope.

bone cancer: Any of several cancers of the skeletal system, such as *osteosarcoma* (q.v.).

Boxer cardiomyopathy (BCM): Technically called Arrhythmic Right Ventricular Cardiomyopathy (ARVC), this is a genetic disease of the cardiac (heart) muscle and largely restricted to Boxers. Often the first symptom is sudden death. In less severe cases, it can be detected with EKGs and treated with medication. Because it is caused by a single dominant gene, any animal that carries the gene will have the disease. It is therefore crucial to screen all breeding stock and under no circumstances breed an afflicted dog.

brachycephalic syndrome: Also called brachycephalic respiratory syndrome; congenital obstructive upper-airway disease; and brachycephalic airway obstruction syndrome (BAOS), this refers to any of a number of upper airway conditions that restrict the flow of air. See *elongated soft palate*, *hypoplastic trachea*, *stenotic nares*.

breathing problems: Difficulty in breathing, which can be due to obstruction, trauma, or disease. See *brachycephalic syndrome*, *collapsing trachea*.

cancer: As in humans and other animals, an abnormal and uncontrolled growth of tissue. In many cases there are underlying environmental or genetic factors. See *lymphoma*, *hemangiosarcoma*, *osteosarcoma*.

Canine Epileptoid Cramping Syndrome (CECS): Also known as Spike's disease, this is a recently discovered (late1990s) ailment in Border Terriers. Symptoms include cramping and epileptic-like seizures, only the dog remains conscious and alert during the seizure. A genetic base is suspected. Treatment is guesswork, with anti-cramping drugs helping some victims.

canine leukocyte adhesion deficiency (CLAD): A primary immunodeficiency caused by an autosomal recessive gene. Found in Irish Setters, this condition causes the white blood cells to be unable to fight infection. Symptoms include frequent recurrent infections; poor healing; weight loss; and high white blood cell count. In severe cases even antibiotic therapy gives poor results.

canine neuronal ceroid-lipofuscinosis (NCL): Technically a complex of several inherited diseases, or canine neuronal ceroid-lipofuscinoses (NCLs), which all cause degeneration of the central nervous system. Because symptoms (blindness and other neurological problems) resemble those of other neurological disorders, a positive diagnosis is only possible by microscopic examination of the nervous system in necroscopy, as the nerve cells from affected dogs fluoresce under UV light.

cardiomyopathy: An irregularity in the muscle tissue of the heart that can lead to arrhythmia (irregular beating). See *Boxer cardiomyopathy*, *dilated cardiomyopathy*.

cataract: Opacity of the lens in the eye. Amount of visual impairment depends on the severity; complete blindness is possible. Although there are many possible causes, in dogs the two most common are genetics and *diabetes* (q.v.). Treatment with eye drops is sometimes effective. The only cure is surgical removal of the cataract. See *juvenile cataracts, posterior polar cataract (PPC)*.

cerebellar abiotrophy (CA): Also known as cerebellar cortical abiotrophy (CCA), this is a genetic condition that results in the loss of Purkinje cells in the brain, which control movement and coordination. There is no treatment or cure, and affected dogs and their close relatives should not be used for breeding.

cerebellar ataxia: A general term for loss of coordination. It can be hereditary, congenital, or the result of disease or injury. One type is *cerebellar abiotrophy* (q.v.) See *Scottie cramp*.

cervical disk problem: A disorder affecting the vertebrae in the neck. See *cervical vertebral instability*.

cervical vertebral instability: A condition seen in large, fast-growing breeds in which pressure is put on the spinal cord in the neck. Symptoms include pain; wobbly gait; inability to stand; and paralysis. Treatment may involve medication; forced rest (cage rest); and surgery. Also called Wobbler's syndrome.

cherry eye: A prolapse of the tear gland of the nictitating (third) eyelid, which swells into a red mass in the corner of the eye. Certain breeds, such as Bulldogs, are more susceptible than others. Correction requires surgery to re-place the gland, and later in life the dog may require daily eye drops for dry eye.

Chiari-like malformation (CM): Also called caudal occipital malformation syndrome or occipital hypoplasia, this is a malformation of the back of the skull bone, making insufficient room for the cerebellum and obstructing the flow of spinal fluid. It is believed by some to be the underlying cause of *syringomyelia* (q.v.) Extremely common in Cavalier King Charles Spaniels but found in other breeds as well.

Chinese Beagle Syndrome: An inherited condition affecting only Beagles. Defects associated with this problem include muscular, neurological, and skeletal abnormalities. Affected dogs show a broadened skull; widely set, slanted eyes; and shortened outer toes. The dogs wind up standing on the two middle toes, and they show stiffness of the legs.

chondrodysplasia: An inherited disorder of the cartilage caused by a simple recessive gene and causing deformities, especially of the legs. It is part of the breed standard for dogs such as Bassets and Corgis, where it produces the desired dwarfed legs, but in other breeds it can produce crippling deformities.

chronic active hepatitis (CAH): A liver condition typically associated with *copper toxicosis* (q.v.).

chylothorax: The buildup of chyle (a lymphatic fluid) in the area around the heart and lungs. It is a rare condition with many suspected causes and a poor prognosis for affected dogs.

cleft palate: A congenital condition most common in brachycephalic breeds, in which the palate fails to fuse and a hole or slit is present. This can affect soft tissues, producing a "hare lip," or there can be an opening between the mouth and the nasal passages. In mild cases the puppies may do well until they are old enough for cosmetic surgery to repair the defect. In more severe cases the puppy has to be tube fed until old enough for reconstructive surgery. There are many possible causes, both genetic and developmental.

coat funk: A term used most by Alaskan Malamute owners to refer to a condition in which the normal cycle of hair shedding and regrowth stops. The unreplaced guard hairs eventually fade and break off, leaving the dog with only a woolly undercoat.

collapsing trachea: A condition most often seen in toy breeds, in which the cartilage rings of the trachea weaken, causing the trachea to collapse. Symptoms range from coughing to respiratory distress and lack of oxygen. Treatment includes weight loss; cough suppression; and medications to dilate the airways. See *hypoplastic trachea*.

Collie eye anomaly (CEA): A genetic disorder that causes various structural defects in the eyes, including *coloboma* (q.v.) and retinal detachment. In mild cases there is little effect, but severe cases lead to blindness. Affected animals and their close relatives should not be bred.

Collie nose: Also called nasal solar dermatitis, this condition manifests as lesions on unpigmented areas of the face (especially eyelids, lips, and nose). Sunlight exacerbates the condition. There is a genetic component, and severity can be mild to severe. Worst cases produce hemorrhaging or even skin cancer. Prophylactic tattooing of dark pigment onto lightly pigmented tissues is effective.

coloboma: A congenital hole or other defect in a structure of the eye. See *Collie eye anomaly (CEA)*, *iris coloboma*.

color dilution alopecia: An inherited disease associated with dilute hair color (blue and fawn) and seen in certain breeds; the majority of cases are Doberman Pinschers. A type of follicular dysplasia that causes the hair shafts to break. There is no treatment or cure, but secondary infections are common and must be treated. Even dogs with severe hair loss lead otherwise happy lives.

compulsive tail chasing: This behavior may simply be learned—perhaps the behavior was rewarded with laughing or other attention, requiring counter-conditioning to eliminate. It can also be caused by boredom or anxiety, in which case it will cease when the dog's environment is improved. In some cases anti-anxiety medications or drugs to regulate dopamine production are necessary. Finally, tail chasing can be a sign of an epileptic-like seizure. A full medical evaluation will reveal the underlying cause of the compulsion and suggest the appropriate treatment.

congenital deafness: Deafness present from birth. Most significant is an inherited deafness associated with merle or piebald colorations. Blue-eyed dogs are also more likely to be deaf. The genetics of canine deafness is a topic of intense study, and there may be more than one mechanism involved. Deafness is more likely in certain breeds, with Dalmatians being the most frequent sufferers, but even mixed-breed dogs can be affected.

congenital heart disease: Any structural or functional defect of the heart present at birth. See *patent ductus arteriosus*.

congenital stationary night blindness (CSNB): An inherited condition in which the affected dog has night blindness and may have severe to complete loss of daylight vision as well. Most often found in Briards.

copper toxicosis: The accumulation of copper in the body, especially in the liver. There is a genetic cause, at least in some breeds. Affected dogs often do not appear ill until the copper levels are very high and damage to the liver is irreversible. Treatment involves diet and medications. See *chronic active hepatitis (CAH)*.

corneal dystrophy: A group of inherited conditions in which defects in the cornea produce various effects. Depending on the type and severity, vision may or may not be affected; in severe cases extremely painful lesions may develop in the cornea, requiring medication and/or surgery. Affected dogs and their close relatives should not be used for breeding.

craniomandibular osteopathy: A probably inherited condition most common in terriers and found in growing dogs. Excess bone growth in the lower jaw and skull bones causes pain and inability to open the mouth. In severe cases tube feeding may be necessary. Typically medication for swelling and pain will get the puppy through until bone growth ceases at about nine or ten months of age, but severe cases may need surgical intervention to restore sufficient jaw motion.

cruciate ligament injuries: See *anterior cruciate ligament injury*.

cryptorchidism: The failure of one or both testes to descend into the scrotum, which should occur before the age of eight weeks. A dog with two undescended testes is infertile, but with one normal testis a dog is fertile. Nevertheless, all cryptorchids should be castrated both because they are at increased risk for testicular cancer and because the condition is genetic. Related females should also not be used for breeding, as the disorder is inherited from both parents.

crystalline corneal opacity: An inherited condition in which cone-shaped gray crystals develop in the center of the cornea and spread across the eye. There is no treatment, but there also is no pain, and usually the dog does not lose all vision.

Curly Coat Problem: A condition manifested by bilateral baldness, from a few small patches to complete loss of hair, in Curly-Coated Retrievers. Breeders struggle with many problems in striving for the ideal coat for these dogs, and it is often difficult to identify what is normal hair loss or shedding and what is abnormal.

Cushing's syndrome: Also called hyperadrenocorticism, this is a condition in which too much of the adrenal hormone cortisol is present in the body, the opposite of *Addison's* *disease* (q.v.). The three main causes are: a pituitary tumor, usually benign; an adrenal tumor, often malignant; and a side effect of long-term steroid treatment, as for allergies or arthritis.

cyst: A small benign lump that is a sack filled with liquid or semi-solid secretions. Common on the skin are sebaceous cysts associated with the sebaceous glands. Although in themselves harmless, cysts should be checked and monitored, as they can be confused with cancerous lumps, such as *mast cell tumors* (q.v.).

cystinuria: An inherited condition in which cystine and other amino acids are not properly reabsorbed in the kidneys, resulting in cystine in the urine, causing urinary calculi (stones). Although found in many breeds, cystinuria is especially dangerous in Newfoundlands, who exhibit an increased incidence of calculi beginning at a younger age. Treatment involves drugs and/or surgery, and medications may be used to discourage formation of new stones. A blood test is available to screen carriers so that the disease can be eliminated with responsible breeding.

deafness: The inability to hear any sounds. It can be unilateral (affecting one ear only) or bilateral (affecting both ears), and congenital (and sometimes hereditary) or acquired after birth.

degenerative heart valve disease: A gradual loss of function in the heart valves. This broad category describes a range of conditions, including *aortic stenosis* (q.v.), *pulmonary stenosis* (q.v.), and *mitral valve disease (MVD)* (q.v.).

degenerative myelopathy: A progressive degeneration of the spinal cord in older dogs that leads to weakness and finally paralysis of the hind end. There is no cure. Treatment consists of exercise; dietary supplements; and medication. A recessive gene associated with the condition has just (2008) been identified.

dental problems: Malformation or disease of the teeth. See *malocclusion*.

dermatomyositis: An inherited condition primarily of Collies and Shetland Sheepdogs with a high degree of variability in which skin and muscle lesions occur, often first on the face. Often the dog outgrows the disease, which can leave scarring. Severe cases require euthanasia, usually because of the dog's inability to eat or drink. Because the mode of inheritance is unclear and because afflicted dogs may show extremely mild symptoms, affected dogs and all of their close relatives should not be bred.

dermoid sinus: A condition in which embryological separation of the neural tube and the skin is incomplete, leaving a sinus along the back that may or may not connect to the spine. If a dermoid sinus becomes infected, it can lead to meningitis. Draining or infected sinuses can be surgically removed.

diabetes: Its full name is diabetes mellitus, and it is a condition in which insufficient insulin is produced, impairing glucose metabolism and causing high blood sugar levels; excessive thirst; and lethargy. Primarily a disease of older (and primarily female) dogs, an inherited juvenile-onset diabetes does rarely occur. In dogs diabetes is typically controllable only with insulin injections once or twice daily.

dilated cardiomyopathy (DCM): A condition in which the heart becomes dilated (enlarged). It can produce *heart murmur* (q.v.) and congestive heart failure. Its prevalence in certain breeds seems to indicate a genetic component.

distichiasis: A condition in which extra eyelashes grow from an abnormal location in the eye and grow inward toward the eye. The eyelashes irritate and abrade the cornea, producing considerable pain and possible loss of vision. Treatment requires surgery. Affected animals should not be bred. See *trichiasis*.

ear infections: Infections of the ear canal and/or eardrum. Recurrent infections can be a problem in floppy-eared breeds because the ear can trap moisture and dirt underneath it.

ectropion: A condition, usually inherited, in which the eyelid grows outward. Surgery is indicated in severe cases. See *entropion*.

elbow dysplasia: An inherited condition in which the three bones of the elbow do not fit together properly, leading to pain; lameness; bone chips; and ultimately severe arthritis. There may be *osteochondritis dissecans (OCD)* (q.v.) lesions. The disease typically manifests during growth in young, immature, large-breed dogs. Treatment consists of medication and surgery. The sooner the condition is detected and treated, the better the prognosis.

elongated soft palate: A condition typically found in brachycephalic breeds and manifesting in young adult dogs. The defect can interfere with breathing, and noisy breathing and snoring are common early symptoms. Surgery can often correct the problem, and it is part of normal repair of various conditions in *brachycephalic syndrome* (q.v.).

enostosis: Also called panosteitis; "pano;" and puppy limp, this condition of unknown origin typically afflicts the leg bones of growing dogs of large and very large breeds. It produces scarring with the bones, and the pain varies from mild to crippling. Treatment involves medicating for swelling and pain. Dogs normally recover completely after many months. A genetic component is suspected, as is possible viral infection and excessive calcium in the diet.

entropion: A condition, usually inherited, in which the eyelid grows inward. This can cause extreme pain and damage the eye. Surgery is the treatment; modern laser surgery techniques have proved effective. See *ectropion*.

eosinophilic myositis (EM): A type of masticatory muscle myositis (MMM), this is usually an autoimmune disorder in which the immune system targets the masticatory (involved in chewing) muscles. Treatment is with steroids. The condition often recurs.

epilepsy: As in humans, epilepsy in dogs is a brain disorder characterized by seizures, in which the animal is unconscious and demonstrates uncontrolled spasms and movements. There are many causes for this neurological disorder, and the severity and frequency of the seizures vary greatly. Diagnosis consists primarily of ruling out any other causes for seizures. Medication can help control the disease.

exocrine pancreatic insufficiency (EPI): An inherited condition in which the pancreas fails to excrete sufficient digestive enzymes, producing a dog with a healthy appetite who loses weight and is malnourished on the best foods. Treatment includes the addition of pancreatic enzymes to a low-fat, low-fiber diet. In most cases treatment will have to continue for life. This is primarily a disease of German Shepherd Dogs.

eye problems: Disease or defect in the eye. See *cataract*, *cherry eye*, *Collie eye anomaly (CEA)*, *distichiasis*, *ectropion*, *entropion*, *glaucoma*, *iris coloboma*, *pannus*, *Poodle eye*, *uveodermatological syndrome (UDS)*.

eyelash problems: Abnormalities in eyelash growth. See *distichiasis*.

eyelid problems: Disease or defect in the eyelid. See *ectropion*, *entropion*.

factor XI deficiency: An inherited bleeding disorder that is not sex linked, so it is found equally in both sexes. See *hemophilia*.

familial nephropathy: An inherited disorder that produces fatal kidney failure in young dogs. Tests are available to detect sufferers before the first symptoms appear and to identify carriers so that they are not used in breeding programs.

Fanconi syndrome: A disease of the kidneys leading to loss of various chemicals into the urine that should be retained. Symptoms include excessive thirst; excessive urination; weight loss; and poor coat. It can be treated with supplements to make up for some of the chemical loss, but the disease is progressive and usually results in death from kidney failure.

follicular dermatitis: A condition similar to an ingrown hair in which a hair follicle in the skin becomes inflamed. Although careful grooming is generally the only treatment necessary, veterinary intervention may be necessary in severe cases.

follicular dysplasia: A genetic disease that causes structural problems in the hair follicles, leading to hair loss. There are many variants of this condition that differ in the type of hair loss; certain types are more common in some breeds than others.

Glanzmann's thrombasthenia: An inherited disorder in platelet function that causes abnormal bleeding.

glaucoma: An increase in the pressure of the fluid in the eye, which leads to blindness. It can be inherited or acquired. Although humans also suffer glaucoma, there is often little pain, but in dogs there can be extreme pain. Permanent visual damage is usually done by the time obvious symptoms appear, so regular ophthalmological screening is important, especially if a dog breed is known to be prone to the disease. Treatment may involve various therapies, including surgery. See *ocular melanosis*.

globoid cell leukodystrophy: An inherited metabolic disorder that ultimately interrupts the normal production of myelin, leading to a variety of neurological symptoms. There is no cure or treatment. Fortunately, the condition can be detected by a blood test, including in heterozygous carriers, so diligent screening of breeding stock can eliminate the disease.

glycogen storage disease (GSD): A complex inherited carbohydrate metabolism disorder in which excess glycogen is stored in body tissues, resulting in *hypoglycemia* (q.v.) and other imbalances that can affect a number of organs and produce many different symptoms. Found primarily in the German Shepherd Dog, this disease is difficult to diagnose. Treatment consists of controlling the hypoglycemia. Affected dogs who survive until adulthood should never be bred.

heart murmur: The abnormal sound caused by turbulent blood flow in the heart, detectable by stethoscope and caused by improper valve closure. Murmurs are symptomatic in various types of valve disease. See *aortic stenosis*, *mitral valve disease*.

heart problems: Structural or functional defects of the heart. This broad category describes a range of conditions, including *cardiomyopathy* (q.v.), *heart murmur* (q.v.), and *mitral valve disease* (q.v.).

hemangiosarcoma: A cancer that originates in the lining of blood vessels. While it can occur anywhere, it is most common in the spleen. This is a very aggressive cancer, and prognosis is poor for an affected dog. Usually by the time symptoms appear and a diagnosis is made, the cancer has metastasized and there are tumors throughout the body. Even with chemotherapy, most dogs do not survive more than a couple of months.

hemeralopia: Also known as day blindness, this is an inherited defect in the cones of the eye. An affected dog can only see in dim light and is effectively blind in bright conditions. There is no treatment or cure. Affected animals and their close relatives should not be bred.

hemivertebrae: A congenital malformation of one or more vertebrae that do not develop fully. In the tail this produces what is known as a "screw tail," a desired trait in some breeds, but in the spine it can cause neurological problems. Mild cases may be asymptomatic, but severe cases manifest as weakness, incontinence, or paralysis. Surgery to decompress the spine and restructure the vertebrae is required in such cases.

hemolytic anemia: Anemia (low red blood cell count) caused by the destruction of the red cells. This can be caused by toxins, pathogens, and other problems, but it can also be an autoimmune response. In severe cases first aid may involve blood transfusions. Treatment requires determination of the cause. See *autoimmune hemolytic anemia*.

hemophilia: An inherited condition in which blood does not clot normally. There are several types of hemophilia in dogs, and severity ranges from mild (excess bleeding after injury or surgery) to life threatening (severe bleeding in the absence of trauma). These genetic diseases are associated with specific breeds; a particular hemophilia is found in one breed, with a different hemophilia being found in another. The different defects are sometimes referred to by the clotting factor they affect, such as "factor VIII deficiency." Many are sex-linked diseases, so mostly males are affected. Females carry the disease and pass it on to their sons. Some people differentiate between "hemophilia" as the sex-linked conditions and call all of the others by their factor name. All breeding stock should be screened to eliminate these conditions in future generations. Euthanasia or frequent blood transfusions are the traditional responses to bleeding disorders, but drug and gene therapy are being actively explored. The emphasis is on developing reliable tests to determine carrier animals to screen breeding stock. See *hereditary factor VII deficiency*, *factor XI deficiency*, *von Willebrand disease*.

hereditary factor VII deficiency: One of several inherited bleeding disorders, generally producing only a mild bleeding problem. See *hemophilia*.

hereditary myopathy: An inherited condition causing muscle weakness.

hereditary necrotizing myelopathy: An inherited degenerative disease of the spine, similar to human multiple sclerosis. Usually manifests between one and two years of age. There is no cure, and an affected dog will eventually need to be euthanized. By strictly regulating breeding to exclude affected animals and their relatives, Kooikerhondje breeders have greatly decreased the incidence of the disease.

hernia: A weakening or rupture in a muscular wall or membrane permitting body tissues to protrude through that wall. Hernias can develop throughout the body, and only those whose protuberances are just below the skin are visible. See *inguinal hernia*, *umbilical hernia*, and *intervertebral disk disease*.

hip dysplasia: The abnormal development of the hip joint in young dogs. Symptoms include rear limb lameness; difficulty moving; and waddling rear gait. Treatment includes physical therapy and pain relievers. See *Legg-Calve-Perthes disease*.

hives: Raised, circular, itchy patches on the skin caused by an allergic reaction. Hives will disappear when exposure to the allergen stops. Can be treated with medicines, but it is important to determine what the dog is allergic to in order to prevent future occurrences.

hyperkalemia: An excess of potassium in the blood usually caused by the failure of the kidneys to properly excrete it. It may also follow as a side effect of certain drug treatments. Irregular heartbeats often result.

hyperthyroidism: A greater than normal level of the thyroid hormone thyroxin in the blood, causing restlessness; irritability; and weight loss despite a voracious appetite. Not common in dogs, when it does occur it is almost always because of a thyroid carcinoma, a cancer that is treated with medication; surgery; or radioactive iodine treatment.

hypertrophic osteodystrophy (HOD): A condition found in rapidly growing puppies of large breeds, in which the bone along the growth plate of the bones (usually leg) is destroyed. Fever and extreme pain often accompany the disorder. Bouts can recur. Treatment is mainly for the pain and swelling. Although permanent skeletal damage is possible, often the pup outgrows the disease with no deformity.

hypoglycemia: A lower than normal level of glucose in the blood, which can lead to a wide variety of problems. See *diabetes*, *glycogen storage disease (GSD)*.

hypomyelinogenesis: A sex-linked genetic disease in which myelin does not form properly on the nerves, leading to pups with neurological disorders: "tremblers" and "shaky puppies." There is no treatment, but often affected puppies eventually grow the proper myelin sheaths on their nerves, leading to the name "delayed myelination" for this condition. Because it is sex linked, it will be most prevalent in male pups, and females can be carriers; for a female to have the disease, her father has to have it, and her mother has to be a carrier. Responsible breeders will not use affected animals or their relatives in breeding programs.

hypoplasia of dens: In this genetic condition, the pivot of the second cervical vertebra fails to form properly, leading to pressure on the spinal cord. Severity ranges widely, from neck pain to complete paralysis from the neck back.

hypoplastic trachea: A congenital disorder seen most in young brachycephalic dogs, in which the trachea is abnormally narrow. Although the symptoms and care are similar to those of *collapsing trachea* (q.v.), the hypoplastic trachea does not change size as the dog breathes in and out.

hypothyroidism: A lower than normal level of thyroxin in the blood, leading to lethargy and weight gain. A common disease with many possible causes, it is easily treated by daily thyroxin pills.

inguinal hernia: A herniation of abdominal tissues through the inguinal ring—the groin area where the hind leg folds against the body. It is seen most often in nonspayed, middle-aged female dogs. There may be a genetic component. Treatment requires reconstructive surgery and should be performed as quickly as possible to prevent strangulation of the herniated tissues, which can include intestines; bladder; and uterus.

immune disease: A disease involving the immune system and thereby the immune response, for example, *canine leukocyte adhesion deficiency (CLAD)* (q.v.). When the immune system attacks the body's own tissues, it is an *autoimmune disease* (q.v.).

immune-mediated hemolytic anemia (IMHA): See *autoimmune hemolytic anemia (AIHA)*.

immunoproliferative small intestinal disease (IPSID): A genetically based autoimmune inflammatory bowel disease, primarily of Basenjis and causing severe diarrhea; protein imbalances; vomiting; and weight loss. Food allergies are implicated in triggering the problem, and some dogs get relief when put on hypoallergenic diets. Medical treatment uses steroids and antibiotics. There is no cure.

inflammatory bowel disease: Similar to Crohn's disease in humans, inflammatory cells infiltrate bowel tissue. Severity of symptoms—primarily vomiting and diarrhea—depends on the type of inflammatory cells, the location of the inflammation, and the particular case. Cause is unknown, and there is no cure. However, in most cases symptoms can be controlled with diet and medication.

infundibular keratinizing acanthoma: A condition of unknown cause that causes small benign tumors of the skin. Some of the nodules have a pore connecting to the skin surface. Surgical removal is possible, but often they are simply left alone unless there are mitigating factors.

inherited blindness: A genetically transmitted blindness. See *congenital stationary night blindness (CSNB)*, *hemeralopia*.

intervertebral disk disease: The herniation of one or more disks between the vertebrae of the spinal column, putting pressure on the spinal cord. Depending on the location and severity, the ruptured disk can cause pain; weakness; or paralysis of the hind legs.

iris coloboma: A hole or separation in the iris of the eye. Symptom severity varies with the degree of the defect, from a very mild light sensitivity to loss of sight. Surgery may be indicated.

irritable bowel syndrome (IBS): This is a psychosomatic disease in which the large intestine spasms in response to stress. In evaluating stress on a dog, it is important to take the dog's point of view. For example, because dogs find comfort in routine, traveling can be especially stressful for them. Treatment consists of medication to reduce the spasms and trying to eliminate the stress.

itchy skin: Any condition causing itchiness and manifested by the dog scratching and/or biting persistently at the spot, often to the point of irritating or even injuring the skin. See *hives*, *zinc deficiency*.

joint problems: Pain or stiffness in the bone joints can indicate a great variety of problems. See *arthritis*, *hip dysplasia*, *juvenile-onset polyarthritis syndrome*, *Legg-Calve-Perthes disease*, *osteochondritis dissecans (OCD)*, *Shar-Pei Fever*.

juvenile cataracts: Cataracts that develop in dogs under six years old, often at age two to three years. There is probably a genetic component. See *cataracts*.

juvenile-onset polyarthritis syndrome: Similar to juvenile rheumatoid arthritis in humans, this autoimmune condition produces bouts of fever and extreme joint pain in young dogs.

kidney disease: Any defect or disorder in the kidneys. See *amyloidosis*, *cystinuria*, *kidney failure*, *urolithiasis*.

kidney failure: The loss of kidney function for any of a variety of reasons. See *amyloidosis*, *familial nephropathy*, *renal cortical hypoplasia*, *renal dysplasia*.

L-2-hydroxyglutaric aciduria (L-2-HGA): An inherited disorder of Staffordshire Bull Terriers in which elevated levels of L-2-hydroxyglutaric acid accumulate in body fluids. It is a metabolic condition that affects the central nervous system. Symptoms include muscle stiffness or weakness; seizures; and tremors. It is caused by a recessive gene, so dogs can be carriers without showing any symptoms. The disease can be eliminated by testing breeding stock and disqualifying any animals that are carriers.

Legg-Calve-Perthes disease: A condition of necrosis of the femoral head (die-off of the ball part of the hip joint). More often found in smaller dog breeds, and there may be a genetic component. X-ray screening for *hip dysplasia* (q.v.) will usually detect this condition as well. In milder cases medication will bring relief for the pain and lameness, while in more severe cases surgery is necessary to remove the diseased bone.

Lundehund syndrome: A combination of various gastrointestinal problems that affect the dog's ability to absorb nutrients from its food. Found only in the rare Lundehund breed, estimates are that 90 to 100 percent of Lundehunds have the condition. Management of the disease involves a special diet, vitamin B12 shots, and various medications. Severe cases may prove fatal. Any Lundehund should receive blood and fecal tests every six months to monitor for this syndrome.

lymphoma: Also called lymphosarcoma, this is one of the most common cancers in dogs and can affect lymph tissue anywhere in the body. It normally responds to chemotherapy, and although it cannot be cured, it can be controlled. Radiation and surgery are not used for this cancer. Bone marrow transplants, although extremely expensive, are an option.

malabsorption syndrome: The condition in which nutrients are not properly absorbed in the intestines, leading to malnutrition despite a quality diet. Possible causes include infections; *inflammatory bowel disease* (q.v.); and *exocrine pancreatic insufficiency (EPI)* (q.v.).

malocclusion: The abnormal alignment of teeth. In some breeds the standard requires alignment that would be considered malocclusion in other dogs. Unless the malocclusion causes eating problems or injury to the mouth, it is usually left alone except for increased dental care to keep the teeth clean. Both extractions and orthodontics are used to treat severe cases.

mast cell tumor: A common type of skin cancer in dogs, one which responds well to chemotherapy, radiation, and surgery. Immune-modulating drugs are also effective.

MDR-1 gene mutation: A mutation in the multi-drug resistance gene, which encodes the production of P-glycoprotein, which protects the brain from a wide variety of drugs. Dogs with the mutation do not produce the protein and can suffer severe illness or death from any of a long list of common medications, both prescription and over-the-counter. Primarily a condition of Collies and related breeds, the occurrence of the mutation in a population has been found to be as high as 75 percent. A simple DNA test can identify affected animals, which can then be treated with alternate medications.

megaesophagus: A dilation of the esophagus from a loss of normal peristalsis (muscular contractions that move food along the digestive system), causing regurgitation after eating. It is common in dogs with *myasthenia gravis* (q.v.). In some cases it is known to be inherited—in the Miniature Schnauzer it is caused by a dominant gene and in the Wire Fox Terrier by a recessive gene.

mitral dysplasia: A congenital defect in the mitral valve of the heart. See *mitral valve disease (MVD)*.

mitral valve disease (MVD): A progressive degeneration of the mitral valve, detectable at first as a *heart murmur* (q.v.) and leading to pulmonary edema, congestive heart failure, and death. While common in old dogs of all breeds, it is an apparently genetic condition common to certain breeds, most notably Cavalier King Charles Spaniels.

MPS-IIIB: This condition, mucopolysaccharidosis type IIIB (also called Sanfilippo syndrome type IIIB), is caused by a single recessive mutation in Schipperkes. It is similar to Tay-Sachs disease in humans and causes a progressive and eventually fatal degeneration of the brain. First symptoms

appear at one to two years of age, and the dog is typically euthanized within one or two more years. There is no treatment, but both victims and carriers can be identified by a DNA test, so the disease can be eliminated by prudent selection of breeding stock.

musculoskeletal problems: Any defect or disorder involving bones, cartilage, and muscles. See *Chiari-like malformation*, *chondrodysplasia*, *craniomandibular osteopathy*, *elbow dysplasia*, *enostosis*, *hypertrophic osteodystrophy (HOD)*, *Legg-Calve-Perthes disease*, *osteochondritis dissecans (OCD)*.

myasthenia gravis (MG): The condition in which there is a lack of acetylcholine receptors in muscle tissue, causing fatigue and muscle weakness. In congenital MG, the dog is born with a lack of receptors, and in the acquired form, the body's own immune system attacks the receptors.

myelopathy: Any disease of the spinal cord. See *degenerative myelopathy*.

myotonia congenita: An inherited disease in which muscles do not immediately relax after contracting. This causes the animal to stiffen and often fall over. For a minute or so the animal quivers uncontrollably, and then the muscles return to normal. There is no treatment or cure.

obesity: The condition of being extremely overweight; the formation of large fat reserves in body tissues. Proper diet and exercise can prevent or treat obesity in dogs.

ocular melanosis: The abnormal production of pigment in the eyes. Found almost only in Cairn Terriers, this inherited condition causes a buildup of fluid in the eye, leading to increased pressure—*glaucoma* (q.v.)—and ultimate blindness.

oligodontia: An inherited reduction in the number of teeth.

osteochondritis dissecans (OCD): A disease of unknown origin that primarily affects growing dogs of the large breeds, characterized by abnormalities in the cartilage within a joint, causing pain and lameness. Treatment ranges from forced rest to surgical repair of the cartilage. See *elbow dysplasia*.

osteosarcoma: A sarcoma cancer of the bone.

pancreatitis: An inflammation of the pancreas in which the gland's digestive enzymes begin digesting the pancreatic tissues. Common causes in dogs include obesity and ingesting fatty meats. It can also result from chronic kidney disease or obstruction of the pancreatic duct.

pannus: A condition primarily found in German Shepherd Dogs and thought to have an autoimmune basis, characterized by chronic, progressive inflammation of the cornea, causing pigment and blood vessels to grow in the normally transparent tissue and impairing vision. It can be effectively controlled with medication, but typically the medication must continue for life.

patellar luxation: A condition most common in miniature and toy breeds, caused by abnormal movement of the patella (kneecap) and the quadriceps muscle that results in periodic pain and lameness, with a hind leg held up off the ground. Mild cases may need no intervention, and surgery is generally very successful in more severe cases. Because there is a suspected genetic component, affected dogs should not be used for breeding.

patent ductus arteriosus (PDA): A congenital condition in which the ductus arteriosus (passage between the pulmonary artery, which carries blood to the lungs, and the aorta, which delivers blood to the rest of the body) does not close at birth. This can lead to pulmonary edema and congestive heart failure. Severe cases require surgery to close the duct.

pemphigus: A collection of autoimmune disorders in which the immune system targets the dog's own skin. Severity ranges from unsightliness to life threatening. Symptoms generally include crusty red sores, and treatment involves lifelong administration of steroids.

persistent pupillary membrane (PPM): The persistence of fetal membranes over the pupil. Normally gone shortly after the puppy's eyes open, remnants may remain. Depending on the severity, there can be very little impairment, sometimes just small cataracts that do not grow larger, but severe cases can cause blindness.

phosphofructokinase (PFK) deficiency: An inherited disorder primarily of various spaniel breeds in which glucose is not properly metabolized to produce energy. A test is available to identify carriers so that they will not be bred.

pituitary dwarfism: Dwarfism caused by hypopituitarism, or abnormally low levels of pituitary growth hormone.

Underlying causes include genetics; infections; and tumors. Born at a normal size, pituitary dwarf puppies are evident by a few weeks of age. This type of dwarfism produces dogs of normal conformation—miniaturizations of the normal dog without disproportionate growth of certain body parts, as is found in *chondrodysplasia* (q.v.). Problems in tooth and fur growth, however, are typical. Although hormone treatment can ameliorate the condition if started as soon as the dwarfism is noticed, it is extremely expensive. This type of dwarfism is well known in German Shepherds.

polyneuropathy: Any disease that affects multiple nerves. It may be inherited or acquired.

Poodle eye: Brown staining of the fur under the eyes from excessive tearing. The exact cause or causes are unknown. Treatments include special grooming, drug therapy, and surgery in extreme cases.

portosystemic shunts: Blood vessels that bypass the liver, sending unfiltered blood back to the heart for distribution to the whole body. They can be a persistence of fetal shunts or extra vessels that grow after birth. Untreated shunts will cause death from liver failure. Some dogs can be stabilized with medication, but surgical correction of the disorder is often necessary. Some cases of shunts are not candidates for surgery, however.

posterior polar cataract (PPC): A probably hereditary cataract that forms on the posterior of the lens in the eye. Such cataracts are generally minor and do not lead to blindness.

primary hyperparathyroidism (PHPT): A condition in which there is excess production of parathyroid hormone due to a lesion in the parathyroid gland. The excess hormone causes an abnormal excretion of phosphorus and retention of calcium in the kidneys. Low phosphorus levels lead to bone resorption. Surgical removal of the lesions is the typical treatment.

primary lens luxation: A probably inherited condition in which the lens of the eye moves from its proper place in the adult dog. If it moves forward, extreme and rapid increase in pressure within the eye (*glaucoma* [q.v.]) can lead to blindness in as little as a few hours. If it moves backward, clouding of the eye is usually the most obvious sign, and treatment is usually with eye drops.

progressive retinal atrophy (PRA): A common inherited disease that eventually causes blindness. Often the dog first develops night blindness, followed by total blindness. There is no treatment, but affected dogs often compensate quite well if not put in novel environments.

prostate disease: Any disorder involving the prostate gland, which is found only in male dogs. Prostate problems include enlargement (hypoplasia); infection (prostatitis); and cancer. Castration (neutering) before puberty prevents the gland from growing and greatly reduces the chance of problems later in life—usually but not always around the age of eight years. Castration is also part of the treatment when intact dogs develop prostate problems. No prostate disorders are easy to treat, and prognosis is not good. This makes neutering of all male dogs not in a breeding program an extremely sound investment in the animals' lifelong health.

protein-losing enteropathy (PLE): Any condition of the intestines that permits proteins into the digestive tract. A wide variety of disorders can cause PLE, including lymphatic or intestinal blockage; intestinal infection or inflammation; foreign bodies; congestive heart failure; and cancer. Weight loss and malnutrition despite a healthy appetite are typical symptoms. There is usually no cure, and treatment depends on the underlying cause. Affected dogs and close relatives should not be bred. See *protein-losing nephropathy (PLN)*.

protein-losing nephropathy (PLN): A condition in which proteins are lost through the kidneys into the urine. As with *protein-losing enteropathy (PLE)* (q.v.), the dog suffers from essential nutrients being lost in the wastes. There is no cure, and treatment focuses on preventing kidney failure and involves special diets as well as medication. Affected dogs and close relatives should not be bred.

Pug Dog Encephalitis (PDE): A disease primarily of Pugs and of unknown cause. It is characterized by inflammation of brain tissues. Symptoms can include seizures; difficulty walking; and blindness. Because symptoms are the same as for other central nervous system diseases (such as rabies, poisoning, distemper), diagnosis is often made during necroscopy. There is no treatment or cure.

pulmonary stenosis: A narrowing of or near the pulmonary valve in the heart, restricting flow of blood from the heart to the lungs. In severe cases this will cause congestive heart failure. Treatments include medications and surgery.

pyometra: A life-threatening condition in which hormonal imbalances cause dilation of the uterus, which then typically becomes infected and filled with pus. If the uterus ruptures before it can be removed, the prognosis is extremely poor for the bitch. Spayed females, obviously, cannot suffer this disorder.

renal cortical hypoplasia: An inherited congenital condition in which the cortex (outer part) of the kidney fails to develop normally and is undersized, leading to kidney failure.

renal dysplasia: An inherited congenital condition in which the normal cellular differentiation in the kidney fails to take place, leading to kidney failure in the most severe cases. The kidney may or may not be normal size.

reproductive problems: Any disease or defect in the reproductive system of a male or female dog, ranging from minor problems to complete sterility.

respiratory problems: Any defects or disorders in the respiratory (breathing) system. See *brachycephalic syndrome*.

retinal dysplasia: A probably inherited congenital condition in which the retina fails to develop properly. Depending on severity, symptoms range from none to complete blindness. There is no treatment, and affected dogs and close relatives should not be used for breeding.

Samoyed hereditary glomerulopathy: A disease of the kidney's glomeruli caused by a sex-linked dominant gene. The defect permits proteins to pass into the urine. Males become ill at 3 months of age and die by age 15 months. Carrier females also show symptoms, but later, and if kidney failure does occur, it happens later in life. This, of course, permits carriers to produce puppies, maintaining the disease in the population. Because it is caused by a dominant gene, it can be eliminated in one generation if affected animals are never bred.

Scottie cramp: A condition in Scotties in which movement is affected. It usually begins as clumsiness and proceeds to lameness, and it can come and go. Although thought by some to be a form of *cerebellar ataxia* (q.v.), others disagree.

sebaceous adenitis (SA): An apparently inherited condition that causes the inflammation and ultimate destruction of the skin's sebaceous glands. The effect is cosmetic rather than health damaging and can range from very minor and detectable only by skin biopsy to severe hair loss and scaling of the skin. Treatment has variable success and involves diet, medication, and grooming.

seizures: Any neurological event characterized by uncontrolled firing of neurons in the brain. They can be caused by genetics; trauma; poisoning; or infections. They can range in seriousness from a temporary staring into space to a violent, thrashing seizure that continues for more than five minutes. The latter is a veterinary emergency, whatever the cause. See *Canine Epileptoid Cramping Syndrome (CECS), epilepsy.*

sensorineural deafness: Deafness caused by defect or damage in the nerves of the inner ear. In congenital sensorineural deafness, the nerves die due to restricted blood flow to the inner ear in the first few weeks after birth. See *congenital deafness.*

Shar-Pei Fever: Also called "Familial Shar-Pei Fever (FSF)" and "Swollen Hock Syndrome (SHS)," this condition affects Chinese Shar-Pei and dogs with Shar-Pei ancestry and is believed to be caused by a single recessive gene. It results in recurrent bouts of fever and joint inflammation, as well as the deposition of amyloid protein in the kidneys, which results in kidney failure. Fever and joint pain can be treated with nonsteroidal anti-inflammatory drugs, and a veterinarian may want to give prophylactic treatment for kidney problems. See *amyloidosis.*

skin allergies: Dogs most frequently manifest allergies as a dermatological rash, although they can occasionally have hay fever-like symptoms. See *allergies, hives.*

skin infections: Any infection involving the skin, which may or may not be associated with a *skin rash* (q.v.). Severity ranges from a small infection to a major problem, such as *sebaceous adenitis (SA)* (q.v.).

skin problems: Dogs can suffer from a wide variety of problems involving the skin. See *Collie nose, cyst, dermoid sinus, hives, infundibular keratinizing acanthoma, itchy skin, mast cell tumor, pemphigus, sebaceous adenitis (SA), skin allergies.*

skin rash: A red, raised, or scaly rash anywhere on the dog's skin. See *allergies, hives, pemphigus, zinc deficiency.*

spina bifida: A congenital condition in which one or more vertebral arches fail to close over the spinal cord. It can be inherited or developmental and is most common in Bulldogs. Similar to *syringomyelia* (q.v.) in its effects.

spinocerebellar ataxia: Also called hereditary ataxia, this inherited condition is characterized by progressive loss of coordination. Although similar to *cerebellar ataxia* (q.v.), this disease has a later onset and is not as serious.

stenotic nares: A narrowing of the nares (nostrils), part of *brachycephalic syndrome* (q.v.). In serious cases, surgery is required.

subaortic stenosis (SAS): Fibrous tissue just below the aortic valve. This condition is common in certain large breeds, including the Boxer and Newfoundland.

syringomyelia (SM): A congenital condition in which fluid-filled cavities form within the spinal cord. Thought to be caused by *Chiari-like malformation* (q.v.). Although it is very different from *spina bifida* (q.v.), due to the damage to the spinal cord, it is similar in its effects.

tetralogy of Fallot (TOF): A quartet of congenital heart defects that are found together. The tetralogy comprises: overriding aorta, *pulmonary stenosis* (q.v.), right ventricular hypertrophy, and ventricular septal defect (VSD). These four defects severely limit the amount of oxygen in the dog's arterial blood, and they stress the heart as it labors to perform with the restrictions caused by the defects. The severity of the symptoms varies individually. The only treatment is surgery to attempt to repair the defects, and it can be moderately successful, although the patient may still succumb to heart failure later down the road.

thrombocytopathy: Any blood clotting disorder caused by dysfunction of the platelets. See *Glanzmann's thrombasthenia, thrombopathia.*

thrombopathia: A bleeding disorder caused by a single recessive gene. A type of *thrombocytopathy* (q.v.).

thyroid problems: Disorders involving the thyroid. See *hyperthyroidism, hypothyroidism.*

toe cancer: Cancer of the toe is often first noticed when the nail is lost. These cancers can be very aggressive, and amputation of the affected toe is the only suitable response. They are most commonly found on large, black dogs such as Standard Poodles.

trichiasis: A condition in which eyelashes grow in the wrong direction and rub against the cornea or the conjunctiva of the eye. This can be caused by infection or inflammation or by injury to the eyelid. Treatment with topical medicines is satisfactory in mild cases; severe cases require surgery. See *distichiasis*.

tumor: A mass caused by the abnormal growth of tissues. A tumor can be malignant (cancer) or benign. "Benign" is a bit of a misnomer because the noncancerous mass can be life threatening if its size or position hamper the proper function of vital organs. If the veterinarian indicates that a tumor is benign and poses no danger, it can be left alone; otherwise, surgery will be required to reduce or remove it. Cancerous tumors are treated the same way as they are in humans—chemotherapy, radiation, surgery.

ulcerative keratitis: Corneal ulcers from any cause, most often trauma or infection. Mild cases can heal on their own, but severe ulcers may require surgical intervention. See *corneal dystrophy*, *distichiasis*, *entropion*.

umbilical hernia: A hernia of the umbilicus (belly button), in which the gap permits abdominal tissues to bulge out at the site. Simple surgery is usually sufficient to correct the problem. There may be an inherited tendency to develop an umbilical hernia.

urolithiasis: The presence of uroliths, or stones in the urinary tract: kidney, ureter, bladder, urethra. The stones vary in composition, and treatment depends on the type of stones present. When a stone completely blocks the passage of urine, it is an emergent, life-threatening situation. See *cystinuria*.

urologic problem: Any problem with the urinary system. See *cystinuria*, *urolithiasis*.

uveodermatological syndrome (UDS): Sometimes called Vogt-Koyanagi-Harada-like syndrome after the human condition VKH syndrome, an autoimmune disease in which the body's immune response is directed at melanin-producing cells. The major symptoms are uveitis (inflammation of the eyes) and loss of pigment. Black dogs may turn completely white. Almost exclusively a disease of Akitas, the syndrome almost certainly has a genetic basis. Visual problems range from bloodshot eyes to blindness and can usually be treated medically if caught in time.

vaccine sensitivity: An allergic reaction to a vaccination. Can be as mild as a swelling at the injection site or as severe as life-threatening anaphylaxis. Some breeds are more susceptible, but any dog (just as any human being) can have an allergic reaction to a vaccination. Because prior exposure is necessary for an allergic reaction, the problem will be seen with a second, third, or later vaccination.

von Willebrand disease: A type of *hemophilia* (q.v.) associated with blood clotting factor VIII.

white shaker dog syndrome: Given this name for historical reasons, the condition is also—and more accurately—known as steroid responsive tremor syndrome and is characterized by generalized head and body tremors with no discernible underlying cause that respond to steroid treatment. More common in small breeds, it can affect dogs of any coat color. Normally diagnosed by ruling out other possible causes, the cause is unknown, although both genetics and an autoimmune response have been suggested.

zinc deficiency: A lack of zinc in the dog's diet that often causes scaly, itchy skin rashes. Symptoms—redness; loss of hair; crusty scales; lesions—are very similar to several unrelated problems, including mange, which must be ruled out, usually by a skin biopsy.

RESOURCES

ASSOCIATIONS AND ORGANIZATIONS

Breed Clubs

American Kennel Club (AKC)
8051 Arco Corporate Drive, Suite 100
Raleigh, NC 27617-3390
Telephone: (919) 233-9767
Fax: (919) 233-3627
E-Mail: info@akc.org
www.akc.org

Canadian Kennel Club (CKC)
200 Ronson Drive, Suite 400
Etobicoke, Ontario M9W 5Z9
Telephone: (416) 675-5511
Fax: (416) 675-6506
E-Mail: information@ckc.ca
www.ckc.ca

**Fédération Cynologique
Internationale (FCI)**
FCI Office
Place Albert 1er, 13
B – 6530 Thuin
Belgique
Telephone: +32 71 59.12.38
Fax: +32 71 59.22.29
www.fci.be

The Kennel Club
1-5 Clarges Street, Piccadilly, London
W1J 8AB
Telephone: 0844 463 3980
Fax: 020 7518 1028
www.thekennelclub.org.uk

United Kennel Club (UKC)
100 E. Kilgore Road
Kalamazoo, MI 49002-5584
Telephone: (269) 343-9020
Fax: (269) 343-7037
www.ukcdogs.com

Pet Sitters

**National Association of
Professional Pet Sitters (NAPPS)**
15000 Commerce Parkway, Suite C
Mt. Laurel, New Jersey 08054
Telephone: (856) 439-0324
Fax: (856) 439-0525
E-Mail: napps@petsitters.org
www.petsitters.org

Pet Sitters International
201 East King Street
King, NC 27021-9161
Telephone: (336) 983-9222
Fax: (336) 983-5266
E-Mail: info@petsit.com
www.petsit.com

Rescue Organizations and Animal Welfare Groups

American Humane Association
1400 16th Street NW, Suite 360
Washington, DC 20036
Telephone: (800) 227-4645
E-Mail: info@americanhumane.org
www.americanhumane.org

American Society for the Prevention of Cruelty to Animals (ASPCA)
424 E. 92nd Street
New York, NY 10128-6804
Telephone: (212) 876-7700
www.aspca.org

Royal Society for the Prevention of Cruelty to Animals (RSPCA)
RSPCA Advice Team
Wilberforce Way
Southwater
Horsham
West Sussex
RH13 9RS
United Kingdom
Telephone: 0300 1234 999
www.rspca.org.uk

Sports

International Agility Link (IAL)
85 Blackwall Road
Chuwar, Queensland
Australia 4306
Telephone: 61 (07) 3202 2361
Fax: 61 (07) 3281 6872
E-Mail: steve@agilityclick.com
www.agilityclick.com/~ial/

The North American Dog Agility Council (NADAC)
24605 Dodds Rd.
Bend, Oregon 97701
www.nadac.com

North American Flyball Association (NAFA)
1333 West Devon Avenue, #512
Chicago, IL 60660
Telephone: (800) 318-6312
Fax: (800) 318-6312
E-Mail: flyball@flyball.org
www.flyball.org

United States Dog Agility Association (USDAA)
P.O. Box 850955
Richardson, TX 75085
Telephone: (972) 487-2200
Fax: (972) 231-9700
www.usdaa.com

The World Canine Freestyle Organization, Inc.
P.O. Box 350122
Brooklyn, NY 11235
Telephone: (718) 332-8336
Fax: (718) 646-2686
E-Mail: WCFODOGS@aol.com
www.worldcaninefreestyle.org

Therapy

Pet Partners
875 124th Ave, NE, Suite 101
Bellevue, WA 98005
Telephone: (425) 679-5500
Fax: (425) 679-5539
E-Mail: info@petpartners.org
www.petpartners.org

Therapy Dogs Inc.
P.O. Box 20227
Cheyenne, WY 82003
Telephone: (877) 843-7364
Fax: (307) 638-2079
E-Mail: therapydogsinc@qwestoffice.net
www.therapydogs.com

Therapy Dogs International (TDI)
88 Bartley Road
Flanders, NJ 07836
Telephone: (973) 252-9800
Fax: (973) 252-7171
E-Mail: tdi@gti.net
www.tdi-dog.org

Training

American College of Veterinary Behaviorists (ACVB)
College of Veterinary Medicine, 4474 TAMU
Texas A&M University
College Station, Texas 77843-4474
www.dacvb.org

American Kennel Club Canine Health Foundation, Inc. (CHF)
P. O. Box 900061
Raleigh, NC 27675
Telephone: (888) 682-9696
Fax: (919) 334-4011
www.akcchf.org

Association of Professional Dog Trainers (APDT)
104 South Calhoun Street
Greenville, SC 29601
Telephone: (800) PET-DOGS
Fax: (864) 331-0767
E-Mail: information@apdt.com
www.apdt.com

International Association of Animal Behavior Consultants (IAABC)
565 Callery Road
Cranberry Township, PA 16066
E-Mail: info@iaabc.org
www.iaabc.org

National Association of Dog Obedience Instructors (NADOI)
7910 Picador Drive
Houston, TX 77083-4918
Telephone: (972) 296-1196
E-Mail: info@nadoi.org
www.nadoi.org

Veterinary and Health Resources

The Academy of Veterinary Homeopathy (AVH)
P. O. Box 232282
Leucadia, CA 92023-2282
Telephone: (866) 652-1590
Fax: (866) 652-1590
www.theavh.org

American Academy of Veterinary Acupuncture (AAVA)
P.O. Box 1058
Glastonbury, CT 06033
Telephone: (860) 632-9911
www.aava.org

American Animal Hospital Association (AAHA)
12575 W. Bayaud Ave.
Lakewood, CO 80228
Telephone: (303) 986-2800
Fax: (303) 986-1700
E-Mail: info@aahanet.org
www.aahanet.org

American College of Veterinary Internal Medicine (ACVIM)
1997 Wadsworth Blvd., Suite A
Lakewood, CO 80214-5293
Telephone: 303-231-9933
Telephone (US or Canada): (800) 245-9081
Fax: (303) 231-0880
E-Mail: ACVIM@ACVIM.org
www.acvim.org

American College of Veterinary Ophthalmologists (ACVO)
P.O. Box 1311
Meridian, ID 83860
Telephone: (208) 466-7624
Fax: (208) 466-7693
E-Mail: office13@acvo.com
www.acvo.org

American Heartworm Society (AHS)
P.O. Box 8266
Wilmington, DE 19803-8266
E-Mail: info@heartwormsociety.org
www.heartwormsociety.org

American Holistic Veterinary Medical Association (AHVMA)
P. O. Box 630
Abingdon, MD 21009-0630
Telephone: (410) 569-0795
Fax: (410) 569-2346
E-Mail: office@ahvma.org
www.ahvma.org

American Veterinary Medical Association (AVMA)
1931 North Meacham Road, Suite 100
Schaumburg, IL 60173-4360
Telephone: (800) 248-2862
Fax: (847) 925-1329
www.avma.org

ASPCA Animal Poison Control Center
Telephone: (888) 426-4435
www.aspca.org

British Veterinary Association (BVA)

7 Mansfield Street
London
W1G 9NQ
Telephone: 020 7636 6541
Fax: 020 7908 6349
E-Mail: bvahq@bva.co.uk
www.bva.co.uk

Canine Eye Registration Foundation (CERF)

P.O. Box 199
Rantoul, Il 61866-0199
Telephone: (217) 693-4800
Fax: (217) 693-4801
E-Mail: CERF@vmdb.org
www.vmdb.org

Orthopedic Foundation for Animals (OFA)

2300 E. Nifong Boulevard
Columbia, MO 65201-3806
Telephone: (573) 442-0418
Fax: (573) 875-5073
E-Mail: ofa@offa.org
www.offa.org

US Food and Drug Administration Center for Veterinary Medicine (CVM)

7519 Standish Place
HFV-12
Rockville, MD 20855
Telephone: (240) 276-9300
E-Mail: AskCVM@fda.hhs.gov
www.fda.gov/AnimalVeterinary/

PUBLICATIONS

Books

Anderson, Teoti. *Dog Training*. Neptune City: TFH Publications, Inc., 2014.

Kennedy, Stacy. *Complete Guide to Puppy Care*. Neptune City: TFH Publications, Inc., 2012.

Morgan, Diane. *Complete Guide to Dog Care*. Neptune City: TFH Publications, Inc., 2011.

Morgan, Diane: *Complete Guide to Dog Breeds*. Neptune City: TFH Publications, Inc., 2014.

Websites

Nylabone
www.nylabone.com

TFH Publications, Inc.
www.tfh.com

INDEX

PHOTOS

Aliaksei Smalenski (Shutterstock.com): 80
Ammit Jack (Shutterstock.com): 108
Andresr (Shutterstock.com): 43, 59, 85, 136, 170
AnetaPics (Shutterstock.com): 4/5
Anna Hoychuk (Shutterstock.com): 118
Anneka (Shutterstock.com): 104
Annette Shaff (Shutterstock.com): 195
AntonioDiaz (Shutterstock.com): 192
Antonio Gravante (Shutterstock.com): 135
atiger (Shutterstock.com): 75
AVAVA (Shutterstock.com): 68
Barna Tanko (Shutterstock.com): 60, 188
Beauty photographer (Shutterstock.com): 40
bikeriderlondon (Shutterstock.com): 72, 160
bitt24 (Shutterstock.com): 56
BoulderPhoto (Shutterstock.com): 148
Canon Boy (Shutterstock.com): 114/115
cappi Thompson (Shutterstock.com): 181
Christian Mueller (Shutterstock.com): 8, 125, 154
Christin Lola (Shutterstock.com): 146
Chutima Chaochaiya (Shutterstock.com): 175
CoolR (Shutterstock.com): 226
cynoclub (Shutterstock.com): 50, 163, 174
Denys Kurbatov (Shutterstock.com): 44
dexter_cz (Shutterstock.com): 114
dezi (Shutterstock.com): 10, 115
Diana Taliun (Shutterstock.com): 130
Dmitry Kalinovsky (Shutterstock.com): 122, 205
dogboxstudio (Shutterstock.com): 105
Dora Zett (Shutterstock.com): 190/191, 194
Dorottya Mathe (Shutterstock.com): 76, 207
Dragon Images (Shutterstock.com): 126
eAlisa (Shutterstock.com): 18
Eric Isselee (Shutterstock.com): front cover, 1, 3 (top right), 3 (lower-middle right), 98, 213
Erik Lam (Shutterstock.com): 9, 110
Ermolaev Alexander (Shutterstock.com): back cover (right)
fluke samed (Shutterstock.com): 224
Footsore Fotography (Shutterstock.com): 212
Fotyma (Shutterstock.com): 150
gabczi (Shutterstock.com): 145
Gelpi JM (Shutterstock.com): 22
George Hoffman (Shutterstock.com): 143
Goodluz (Shutterstock.com): 139
gorillaimages (Shutterstock.com): 11, 142, 159
GVictoria (Shutterstock.com): 39, 55 (top right)

Halfpoint (Shutterstock.com): 121
Igor Normann (Shutterstock.com): 172, 208
Imfoto (Shutterstock.com): 70
improvise (Shutterstock.com): 203
Inna Astakhova (Shutterstock.com): 131
iravgustin (Shutterstock.com): 189
Irina oxilixo Danilova (Shutterstock.com): 64/65
Jack Jelly (Shutterstock.com): 55 (bottom left)
jadimages (Shutterstock.com): 204
Jagodka (Shutterstock.com): back cover (left)
Jaromir Chalabala (Shutterstock.com): 102, 176
J. Bicking (Shutterstock.com): 228
Jeanette Dietl (Shutterstock.com): 171
Jeff Thrower (Shutterstock.com): 183
Jim DeLillo (Shutterstock.com): 29
Kankaitom (Shutterstock.com): 83
Karen Walker (Shutterstock.com): 210
Khakimullin Aleksandr (Shutterstock.com): 84, 198
Kirill Konstantinov (Shutterstock.com): 44/45
Koncz (Shutterstock.com): 156
Ksenia Raykova (Shutterstock.com): 4 (left), 14, 45, 162
Kuttelvaserova Stuchelova (Shutterstock.com): left flap (bottom)
Lenkadan (Shutterstock.com): 37
leungchopan (Shutterstock.com): 182
L.F (Shutterstock.com): 58, 165
Lindsay Helms (Shutterstock.com): 120
Ljupco Smokovski (Shutterstock.com): 28
Lori B.K. Mann (Shutterstock.com): 30
Makarova Viktoria (Shutterstock.com): 96
MANDY GODBEHEAR (Shutterstock.com): 113
Marie C Fields (Shutterstock.com): 52
marilyn barbone (Shutterstock.com): 186
mdmmikle (Shutterstock.com): 127
MeePoohyaPhoto (Shutterstock.com): 164
mezzotint (Shutterstock.com): 91
Michelle D. Milliman (Shutterstock.com): 107
Mike Dexter (Shutterstock.com): 151
Mikkel Bigandt (Shutterstock.com): 218
Monika Wisniewska (Shutterstock.com): 46/47, 66, 124
Muh (Shutterstock.com): 197
nata-lunata (Shutterstock.com): 128
Nejron Photo (Shutterstock.com): 129
N K (Shutterstock.com): 132
Oleg Malyshev (Shutterstock.com): 31
otsphoto (Shutterstock.com): 187, 196
Patryk Kosmider (Shutterstock.com): 34
Petr Jilek (Shutterstock.com): 86/87, 152/153
phoebe (Shutterstock.com): 219
Photographee.eu (Shutterstock.com): 184, 200

photomim (Shutterstock.com): 6/7
Ratikova (Shutterstock.com): 109
Reddogs (Shutterstock.com): 36, 214
Rita Kochmarjova (Shutterstock.com): 13, 24/25, 116/117, 149
Robert Neumann (Shutterstock.com): 49
Rob van Esch (Shutterstock.com): 5 (right)
Rock and Wasp (Shutterstock.com): 88
Roger costa morera (Shutterstock.com): 133
Sam Strickler (Shutterstock.com): 180
Sari ONeal (Shutterstock.com): 41
Scorpp (Shutterstock.com): 74
Sean Locke Photography (Shutterstock.com): 138
Sergey Nivens (Shutterstock.com): 71, 157
Sheeva1 (Shutterstock.com): 92
Shutterstock.com: 111
Soloviova Liudmyla (Shutterstock.com): 147, 179
Sudarat Thayom (Shutterstock.com): 3 (bottom right)
Susan Schmitz (Shutterstock.com): 3 (bottom left)
Sutichak Yachiangkham (Shutterstock.com): 20
Svetlana Valoueva (Shutterstock.com): 155, 216/217
Tatiana Katsai (Shutterstock.com): 54, 79, 90
Tatyana Vyc (Shutterstock.com): 103
The Len (Shutterstock.com): 78
Tyler Olson (Shutterstock.com): 178
Vera Zinkova (Shutterstock.com): 81
violetblue (Shutterstock.com): 100
Vitaly Titov & Maria Sidelnikova (Shutterstock.com): 26, 211
V. J. Matthew (Shutterstock.com): 63
VP Photo Studio (Shutterstock.com): 168, 199
Whytock (Shutterstock.com): 112
WilleeCole Photography (Shutterstock.com): 3 (upper-middle right), 97, 99, 134, 202
Ysbrand Cosijn (Shutterstock.com): 220, 221, 222
Zuzana UhlÃ€kovÃ¡ (Shutterstock.com): 141

All other photos courtesy of Isabelle Francais and TFH archives

ABOUT THE AUTHOR

Eve Adamson is a six-time *New York Times* best-selling author who has written or co-written more than 65 books, including Animal Planet *Complete Guide to Dog Grooming*. For many years, she served as a contributing editor for *Dog Fancy* magazine and a columnist for *AKC Family Dog* magazine. In 2013, she was inducted into the Dog Writers Association of America (DWAA) Hall of Fame. Eve lives in Iowa City with her family, including her dogs, Jack and Sally. To find out more about Eve, visit her website at www.eveadamson.com.

At Animal Planet, we're committed to providing quality products designed to help your pets live long, healthy, and happy lives.